ANECDOTE
&
EVIDENCE

---

*Essays Linking Social Research
with Personal Experience*

Richard Katzev

Library of Congress Number: 2002091456
ISBN: Softcover   1-4010-5432-3

This book was printed in the United States of America.

To order additional copies of this book, contact:
Xlibris Corporation
1-888-795-4274
www.Xlibris.com
Orders@Xlibris.com
14991

CONTENTS

PLACES

EXCHANGES

RESEARCH

RECOLLECTIONS

To Aphra,
always

To strive,
to seek, to find, and not to yield.

Ulysses
Alfred Lord Tennyson

PREFACE

What happened to the writer is not what matters;
what matters is the large sense that the writer
is able to make of what happened.

Vivian Gornick

While I have authored a fair number of research reports in psychology, it is only recently that I have decided to try my hand at writing personal essays. Even though the two forms are said to differ, I have combined research evidence with my own experience in several of the essays in this collection. I know this is not commonly done, even though the personal essay is said to be "notoriously flexible." Yet social science research can often render personal experience more intelligible and nothing is gained by continuing to isolate the two from one another.

Phillip Lopate put the matter well in his Introduction to *The Art of the Personal Essay.* "One would like to think that the personal essay represents a kind of basic research on the self, in ways that are allied with science and philosophy." By virtue of predisposition and training, this type of thinking has become almost second nature to me and I hope the essays in this collection illustrate the value and ease of blending research with memoir. Silently, I harbor the wish that it was more widely practiced, in both public discourse and essay writing.

I doubt if I would have ever started these essays were it not for the personal computer and the technology of electronic mail. I really took to the computer, especially to word processing, and I was galvanized by it into a flurry of professional report writing. That was long before the Internet or e-mail and when they arrived, I took to the computer all over again. I found it hard to resist the verbal play and conversational style of e-mail exchanges. In sending e-mails, I suddenly found myself writing far more and with much greater ease than ever before.

Indeed, e-mail messages and personal essays have much in common. Lopate describes the personal essay as conversational, informal, and intimate. E-mails are precisely the same. He says the personal essay is confessional, playful, and honest. So too is e-mail. E-mail is basically a kind of easy-going, rapid-fire version of the personal essay. Writing both is great fun and, at times, even illuminating.

The work of Vivian Gornick has also had a major influence on my writing. Her essays on letter writing, solitude, and the experience of living in the city served as a catalyst for my own reflections on these topics. She writes forcefully, with a powerful emotional eloquence and considerable insight. I am deeply indebted to her work and to her conception of the personal essay as "an attempt to deliver a bit of wisdom by interpreting your own experience around an organizing principle."

Finally, I want to acknowledge the very large and continuing influence of the *New Yorker* magazine. The *New Yorker* introduced me to the world of writing. It made it seem important and demonstrated what clear and accomplished writing can achieve. I try to write as well as those who publish in its pages. What reader doesn't? Yet I have no expectations that anything of mine will ever appear in the magazine.

But I often aspire to unattainable ends. That never deters me from trying and, in this instance, from trying to write intelligently, not because I want to be or am a writer, but simply because at times writing is exhilarating. Harold Bloom said: "One writes to keep going, to keep oneself from going mad . . . ." Clearly one also writes for those occasional moments when it is going well, even if the experience is, in the main, illusory.

Portland, Oregon
February 2002

PLACES

I begin my inward journey by writing about place. Some do so by writing about love, war, suffering, cruelty, power, God or country. I write about place or the memory of place . . . . An exile is not just someone who has lost his home; he is someone who can't find another.

André Aciman

SEARCHING FOR QUERENCIA

Away from neighborhood, away from region, away from nation, we become aware of neighborhood, region, and nation as objects of querencia. But the engagement from which all these larger attachments flow is a personal, specific affection for one's own place ... for some little corner of the world ... that connects us to the world to begin with.

It has been over 20 years since I first remember reading about the Spanish concept of *querencia*. It was in a brief *New Yorker* "Talk of the Town" piece about the state of mind of an English airline pilot as he approached the shores of England at the end of one of his trans-Atlantic flights.[1] The deep green English countryside comforted and restored him each time it appeared on the horizon. "He belonged to England. England was home." The author described *querencia* as the affection a person feels for the place one calls home and the sense of well-being and belonging that such a place gives rise to. You are glad to be there. It nourishes and informs you. You are said to feel at peace in your *querencia*.

I copied this short "Talk of the Town" note, filed it in one of the notebooks I keep and read it over every now and then. Its truth, which I was only dimly aware of at first, became clearer to me at each reading. It is particularly relevant to me now, as I think about leaving the city and the neighborhood that has been my home for the past thirty-five years.

While many people believe Portland, Oregon is one the most livable places in this country and is doing everything right in planning its future, it is also undeniably cold, wet, and dreary here much of the year. Since I am no longer young, I am growing weary of dealing with it or even thinking about it. Yet, I am ambivalent about leaving. In spite of its harsh winters, Portland still has much of what I am looking for in a city and, other than my favorite towns in Europe, I am having difficulty finding another place that feels like it could become my *querencia*.

There was a concert in my neighborhood park the other night. I came upon it unexpectedly during an after-dinner stroll. A small rock band was playing. People were clustered around the bandstand or sitting on the grass. Some were listening to the music. Others were enjoying a picnic dinner. Some were sipping wine and munching chips. Children were running around everywhere, climbing on the large free-form sculptures in the park. Young couples, families, old couples, singles, lovers, quite a heterogeneous bunch were there. After mingling a while with the crowd, I returned home feeling glad, after all, to be here in my neighborhood.

In its narrowest sense, *querencia* refers to the place where one lives, one's home, the place one returns to at the end of a trip. I also think of *querencia* more generally in terms of other places that individuals become attached to—their city, nation or, indeed, their neighborhood. In her book *On Bullfighting*, A. L. Kennedy used the term to describe the bull's preferred spot in the ring, "where a matador cannot enter without extreme risk to himself." She reports that a bull will charge if the matador blocks its return to this place. This usage captures the essence of *querencia*—it is a favored place, it feels safe to be there, and it is comforting to return to.

To be honest, I have never felt much affection for the places where I have lived. Either they were too cold or too culturally impoverished. Above all, none ever felt like home and I knew that eventually I would leave. *Querencia* is not a place you want to leave. During my first visit to Portland, I recall thinking that it was not a place where I would ever want to live. Yet, Portland has been my home for over 30 years now and I have come to feel a certain degree of contentment here. While I still hope to be leaving soon, I realize that in an unexpected way, I have gradually become attached to this place.

Until recently, I had never lived in an urban neighborhood the way it is known in Europe and in most of the larger cities of this country. I was raised in the heart of West Los Angeles, not far from shops and business centers, but still, we always had to get in the car to go anywhere. This has been true of all of the places I have lived since, where even though they were also relatively close to the city center, I have been as isolated and automobile dependent as any suburban resident.

I went out to water the plants in the garden the other night. In a moment or two, I heard a woman's voice call my name.

I had no idea where it was coming from or who it might be. It seemed to be coming from a passing cloud. "How nice your garden looks," the woman said. "I want to tell you how much I enjoy looking out upon your beautiful flowers." I finally located the voice. It came from a woman peering out of her third-floor apartment in the building next to mine. We chatted a bit. She had lost her husband, then a bundle in a business enterprise, as well as her formerly slim figure. But she had not forgotten how to express her appreciation for the colorful flowers growing in my garden pots.

It was only after I had been to Europe a few times that I began to appreciate what it meant to be able to walk most everywhere I wanted to go. In the neighborhoods there, I found merchants, homes, and businesses all clustered within an easy walking distance of one another. Eventually I became aware that the inner core of the northwest area of Portland had gradually become a European-style neighborhood. Almost immediately after moving there, I found for the first time in my life, that I could manage my daily affairs without using my car. I would sometimes go for weeks without driving anywhere. The fact that this is possible, that most everything is no more than a five-or ten-minute walk, means everything to me now.

There is really nothing special about this area of the city. Indeed, it is shabby in spots and the people are not always so lovable. But I am familiar with it, it can meet most of my needs, and everything is relatively close. Apartments and homes, some with lovely gardens, are not far from the shops and bistros, markets and bookstores that dot the area. Instead of driving, I take to the sidewalk to reach them. When I head out on my rounds, I invariably encounter friends and others I have seen before and would like to get to know. I develop a bond with the anonymous people I pass on the street so that heading out becomes a social event that has transformed my mundane chores into silent attachments.

The other day, I walked to Rich's Cigar Store to get some magazines for the long weekend. Since I go there often, it didn't surprise me that I was greeted warmly when I entered. The giggling lady at the counter said she had something for me—a five-dollar bill that I had apparently dropped the last time I was there. I was astonished that she had saved it for me all this time. They don't know my name at Rich's. So the giggly woman told me they had been saving it for the Paris Review *guy. I know they don't carry the* Review, *but I always ask for it anyway when I go there. They had been saving the five-dollar bill for the* Paris Review *guy.*

On warm summer nights, the energy of the streets beckons. The cafes are crowded with long lines of expectant diners. A lucky few are seated at the tables outside. The talk is zestful. The bars and markets, the music and shops are brimming with customers. Young women parade down the street in black sundresses, modeling their tans. It is all very alluring. Who are these people, where have they come from and why are they there? In her essay, "On the Street," Vivian Gornick[2] describes the way the anonymous encounters between strangers on the street turn your thoughts in this direction.

> I see, in the air between me and the crowded horizon, the people of the day. I begin revising the scenes, adding dialogue here, analysis there, commentary further on.... With a start, I realize I am writing the story

of the day, lending shape and texture to the hours just behind me. They're in the room with me now, these people I brushed against today. I'd rather be here with them tonight than with anyone I know. They return the narrative impulse to me.

The neighborhood returns much more. Gornick writes:

> You are never less alone than you are in a crowded street that at times enfolds you so that you do not feel shut out .... There is no one you want to be with as much as the strangers who jostle and bump you on the street.

I went to Powell's the other day. It is said to be one of the largest, if not the largest, bookstores in the country and, wonder of wonders, it is all but three blocks from my home. It was a cool and rainy Saturday. What a crowd, not a single empty table in the large coffee bar, individuals typing on their laptops, others chatting amiably or playing chess. The aisles were filled with book lovers searching intently for their next acquisition or reading one while sitting on the floor. A large group had gathered upstairs for a poetry reading. There were long lines at the checkout stand. It was wonderful to be there. The dreary afternoon was all but forgotten.

My daughter and her family live in the suburbs now, about two miles from the nearest town in a cluster of homes set back about a mile from an eight-lane freeway. Each time I visit, I am struck by the vast differences between their neighborhood and mine. The homogeneity of theirs is conspicuous, with every building a home, and every home a garage, garden, and shake roof. There are no buses, apartment houses, coffee bars or telecom warehouses nearby. Most of the homes scattered about the hillside in their suburban setting face away from the street. There are no sidewalks and it is rare to see anything like the sort of social life that is everywhere along the sidewalks of my urban neighborhood.

In discussing the importance of Jane Jacobs' work on urban design, Malcolm Gladwell describes the urban experiences that are so sorely missing from daily life in the suburbs.

> The miracle of Hudson Street, according to Jacobs, was created by the particular configuration of the streets and buildings of the neighborhood. Jacobs argued that when a neighborhood is oriented toward the street, when sidewalks are used for socializing and play and commerce, the users of that street are transformed by the resulting stimulation: they form relationships and casual contacts they would never have otherwise. The West Village, she pointed out, was blessed with a mixture of houses and apartments and shops and offices and industry, which meant that there were always people "outdoors on different schedules and ... in the place for different purposes." ... Sparely populated suburbs may look appealing, she said, but without an active sidewalk life, without the frequent serendipitous interactions of many different people, "there is no public acquaintanceship, no foundation of public trust, no cross-connections with the necessary people."[3]

There is nothing like a public square or central gathering place in my daughter's suburban enclave. A park that might become one was recently built on the main street of town, a few miles from their home, as well as everyone else's. I have driven by that park many times—it is well beyond a normal stroll, unless you're in the mood for a lengthy hike. Not once have I seen anyone there or even anyone approaching the place. Nor have I seen an area for people to park the cars they must drive to get there. I admire the park, the trees, and benches that have been abundantly distributed throughout. I hope that it will eventually become a popular gathering place. But in all honesty, I have no reason to believe that will happen, as long as you have to strap yourself in your three-ton utility vehicle every time you want to go there.

In truth, my daughter spends a fair amount of each and every day on the road going to and fro on her rounds. In the morning, the kids are driven to their schools, each some distance from the other. At the end of their school day, which is never the same, they are retrieved and then transported to their after-school activity, soccer practice, ballet school or language class. Their market is miles from their house, as is everywhere else they go each day.

In visiting, I have come to understand how the design of homes and streets can so readily give rise to the isolation and alienation reported to exist in the suburbs. The entire setting is far removed from the concept of "the city as a human event." Is it any wonder that American teenagers feel so disconnected from the larger culture when they are raised in such a world? I know that's the way I feel when I am there.

It is said that everyone knows everyone else in a small town. Things are not much different in my neighborhood. It is not uncommon to encounter a friend on the streets. One night last week, I went out for a late-evening stroll. On the way, I bumped into a long-time friend who was returning from an evening concert in the park. I treated him to a cone. The next night, as I was returning from the market, I heard someone pounding on the window of a restaurant that I was passing by. More friends beckoned me in. I stayed to chat with them for a while. Every once in a while, my neighborhood seems like a small town, even though it is in the midst of a big one.

I went to Italy after a recent visit with my daughter and her family. Again I was struck by the lively public socializing that I observed on the streets of the neighborhood in Florence that has almost become my second home. There the people greet each other with great warmth. The owners stand outside their stores in order to better converse with those who own the shops across the way.

I doubt that the rarity of such encounters in America is because Italians are more outgoing than we are. Rather, I think it has more to do with the almost haphazard way their cities have evolved over the centuries and the resulting relationship of the buildings to the street. The frequent socializing of the Italians occurs because their cities naturally invite fortuitous meetings between individuals as they stroll along the sidewalks or visit the piazza in their neighborhood.

Now in Florence, when the air is red with the summer sunset and the campaniles begin to sound vespers and the day's work is done, everyone collects in the piazzas. The steps of Santa Maria del Fiore swarm with men of every rank and every class;

artisans, merchants, teachers, arts, doctors, technicians, poets, scholars. A thousand minds, a thousand arguments; a lively intermingling of questions, problems, news of the latest happening, jokes; an inexhaustible play of language and thought, a vibrant curiosity; the changeable temper of a thousand spirits by whom every object of discussion is broken into an infinity of sense and significations—all these spring into being, and then are spent. And this is the pleasure of the Florentine public.[4]

I think a great deal about the design of neighborhoods when I visit the large urban centers of Europe, even though it is not a subject I have ever studied. I know the European model is not everyone's favorite. But it is mine and I can see how humane it is and how readily it gives rise to the active street life that is all but nonexistent in the cities and towns of this country. A person builds his or her own sense of *querencia* out of those experiences, even when he or she is *anonymous.*

In his book, *Intimate Anonymity,*[5] Hillel Schocken defines a city as: "a fixed place where people can form relations with others at various levels of intimacy, while remaining entirely anonymous." Schocken argues that a city should make it possible for individuals to have contact with a variety of people from whom they can choose their intimates. He concludes his essay by noting: "The future of urbanism lies in the understanding that the city is a human event, not a sculpture." I am sure this is the secret to the design of all good cities and the neighborhoods within them. It is surely the secret of my neighborhood in Portland and why, through the relationships that I form here, some of which are personal, others entirely anonymous, I find myself growing increasingly more attached to it.

The art galleries in my neighborhood hold an open house in the evening on the first Thursday of each month. It has turned out to be a happening, bringing street vendors, musicians, and aspiring artists to the area for the night. Crowds of smartly dressed people promenade from gallery to gallery. The local restaurants are packed. During one such First Thursday, the hair saloon across the way held a fashion show that you might have seen in Milan. This month, the Italian "gastronomia" across the street held an elaborate street fair with tables of food, wine, and cheese. And to everyone's astonishment, the owner had also imported the troupe of Sbandieratori, flag artists of Sansepolcro in Tuscany. The flag wavers were dressed in wonderfully colorful costumes and, after marching through the neighborhood, stopped right outside our front door to perform their complex flag-waving routines accompanied by the steady, rhythmic beat of drums and crystal-clear clarions. The party went on through the evening with much dancing, singing, and milling around and a good deal of conversing in Italian.

Increasingly now when I travel, I find myself searching for *querencia,* for a place where I will be able to experience the feeling that it is said to foster. The quest has not been easy. I have also been thinking about why this pursuit seems so important to me now. What difference does it make where I live? City or country, town or metropolis, I am not going to be any different. Won't I still seek the same experiences, find the same pleasures, and fight the same battles regardless of where I live?

I have no answer to that question. Who does? It is only a matter preference. Preference for a place where there is sun and it is warm enough to walk to the places I like to go. Preference for inviting bistros and coffeehouses where I feel welcome to linger a while; a market with fresh bread, fish, fruit, and vegetables near at hand; and a well-stocked magazine and bookstore, and one or two cinemas not far away. Parks and gardens spread about the area and, if I am really lucky, a library and university close by.

They closed off the street in front of our house the other night. Piazza Italia had arranged our first neighborhood Bocce Ball Tournament. Two courts, each one laid out to precision with a green carpet, covered the asphalt street. At one of end of the block, a banner of flags from the Sienese contradra had been hung. As soon as I saw them, I dashed back home to collect the ones I had bought there several years ago. In due course, they were taped to the parking meters along the street. It was a lovely warm night, the street was mobbed, music was in the air, groups were eating at the outdoor tables, teams were battling on the courts, and the colorful flags from Siena were waving in the breeze. Even the governor and his wife were there. Other than the Borgo S. Jacopo, this was surely the place to be that night.

Notes

1   December 24, 1979, Volume 55, Number 45, pp. 27-28.

2   Vivian Gornick, On the Street, *New Yorker*, September 9, 1996, pp. 72-77.

3   Malcolm Gladwell. Designs for Working. *New Yorker*, December 11, 2000.

4   Richard Goodwin, The American Condition, *New Yorker*, January 28, 1974.

5   *Intimate Anonymity, The Israeli Pavilion*, The 7th International Exhibition of Architecture, The Venice Biennial, Tel Aviv: Kal Press Ltd., 2000.

WAITING FOR THE NEW YORKER

While the magazine certainly provided some readers with a symbolic city, others saw it as a bastion against the forces of cultural decline.

Mary Corey

In May of 2000, the *New Yorker* magazine held a festival in New York to celebrate its 75th Anniversary. Many of its well-known authors read from their work, some lectured and others participated in panel discussions or gave interviews. The Festival was such a success that it was repeated the following year, when, unlike the year before, I was able to attend.

Think of it. The writers of a weekly magazine holding forth about their work during three full days of readings, lectures, and discussions. Outside academic society meetings, I can think of nothing else like it in this country, surely not by any other magazine or periodical. While the audience, which at times numbered in the hundreds, was largely from New York City, many individuals came from other places throughout the nation. I had traveled across the country from Oregon; one woman I met had come all the way from Honolulu.

What led me to travel so far at some expense to attend this festival? No one invited me. The airfare, hotel, meals, and the events themselves were not free. I knew none of the authors or editors of the magazine. The *New Yorker* is only a magazine after all. But, of course, it is far more than that, at least it is for me and many other life-long readers.

I can't be entirely sure when I first started reading the *New Yorker*. Perhaps I was in high school or even before. But I do recall there was always a copy around the house and I know that once I started reading the magazine, I never stopped. This is a tale told by most dedicated readers, including its current editor, David Remnick, who, upon assuming the post, remarked: "I was raised on this magazine."

The arrival of the *New Yorker* is one of the main events of my week. It bothers me when it isn't delivered on time and, if it doesn't arrive the next day, occasionally I will go out to buy a copy at the newsstand. Of course, it usually drifts in the day after that. But I'd rather not run the risk that it won't or, as happens now and then, it will be delivered by mistake to someone else.

With the exception of the recently introduced double issues, the magazine has been published every week for the past seventy-seven years. Frankly, I find this rather astonishing. Putting together a magazine of this quality *week after week* for as many years as this (with no reason to believe it will be any different in the years ahead) seems something of a miracle to me.

You have to stand before the bound volumes of the magazine on the shelves of any major library to really appreciate what this means. When I found myself doing this the other day, I was dumbfounded by the row upon row of back issues of the magazine. Then, as I began my search for a "Talk of the Town" piece that I wanted to cite, I realized I was going through one issue after another, as though it was the latest. Hours later I found the piece I was seeking, although it would have taken but a moment had I not been so caught up in thumbing page by page through the old issues.

Everything was still there. The advertisements for fashionable clothes and exotic places, the hilarious cartoons, the profiles of people-you-always-wanted-to-meet. The essays were longer then, but no less serious, and once they captured your interest, they took forever to finish. The same was true of the "Profiles," the "Letters" posted from European capitals or those unforgettable Pauline Kael film reviews, none of which seemed the least bit dated on rereading.

There were more short stories then and who would not want to reread those that moved you the first time around—Cheever's "The Country Husband," Salinger's "A Perfect Day for Bananafish," William Maxwell's "What He Was Like" or my favorite Munro, "The Jack Randa Hotel." Here still is classic literature about memorable people and situations that continue to bring pleasure and insights about yourself that you had not recognized before.

I can clearly recall the first time I read some of those stories and how I was affected by the experience. To cite an instance, I will never forget the first time I read

Munro's "The Jack Randa Hotel," her comedic tale of a fractured marriage and runaway husband. It was late in the afternoon, the day was warm, and I was in Italy, on the rooftop terrace of the hotel in Florence where I was staying. It was a *perfect moment*. I read her story slowly. Very slowly, as I knew the moment would not last long or be repeated soon, if ever, again.

Like other longtime readers, I go through each issue in a fairly regular fashion. I turn at once to "Table of Contents," also a recent addition, to learn who the writers are and what they have written about. Then I proceed, page by page, through the entire issue for the first time, reviewing the "Talk of the Town," the cartoons, the poems, occasional sidebars and the ads, especially the little ones that appear in column format toward the end of the issue. After a suitable period of restraint, I commence reading a fair amount of each issue.

I have been doing this now with very few exceptions for at least 40 years. Recently I have begun to wonder about the cumulative impact of this experience. How has this steady diet of reading the *New Yorker* influenced the life I lead or the work I do? Granted, this is a difficult question. I'm not sure it can ever be answered. Yet, in a way, isn't it the kind of question we might ask of any aesthetic or intellectual experience? How do the films we see, the books we read, or the theatrical events we attend influence us? These questions have always been difficult to answer.

But a lifelong experience of reading the *New Yorker* is not very different from those experiences and must surely leave an imprint upon its life-long readers. Without any systematic research, there are two approaches one can take in trying to identify the nature of this influence. One can either imagine what a regular reader's life would be like without the magazine or, alternatively, recount in a concrete way how the magazine has shaped the actions they take and beliefs they hold. The first approach would yield a fairly speculative account; in fact, it would probably lead to several. So instead, I will adopt the second, by considering my own experience, since the *New Yorker* has an ongoing and very real place in my life.

As I begin to think about the matter, I realize that I read the magazine much the way I read most written materials. I make comments in the margins, copy notable passages, and duplicate articles that I want to save. An article has more than once motivated me to read more on a topic, undertake a research project or turn my interests in a new direction. I often talk about the articles with friends and students. Some, like John Hersey's *Hiroshima* or Rachel Carson's *Silent Spring* and more recently Malcolm Gladwell's work on the *Tipping Point* have spurred me to action and debate. I will often cite a *New Yorker* essay in the writing I do and, from time to time, refer to them in the lectures I give.

In my social psychology class, to cite one instance, I usually lecture about the effects of violence in the media. The students are always interested in the research on this issue, even if it is inconclusive. In preparing the lecture, I look over the material in my file each year to incorporate the latest studies and review those that I have found the most instructive. In doing so, I always reread Pauline Kael's masterly review of *Bonnie and Clyde* that appeared in the October 21, 1967 issue.

My first thought, of course, is that no one writes movie reviews with that kind of brilliance any more. But I don't speak about that with the students. Instead, I discuss her analysis of the role of violence in the film and show how it anticipated future research findings on the impact of media violence. Kael wrote:

> Such people [those who want to place legal restraints on movie violence] see "Bonnie and Clyde" as a danger to public morality; they think an audience goes to a play or a movie and takes the actions in it as examples for imitation. They look at the world and blame the movies. But if women who are angry with their husbands take it out on the kids, I don't think we can blame "Medea" for it; if, as has been said, we are a nation of mother-lovers, I don't think we can place the blame on "Oedipus Rex."

> The movies may set styles in dress or lovemaking, they may advertise cars or beverages, but art is not examples for imitation . . . People don't "buy" what they see in a movie quite so simply; Louis B. Mayer did not turn us into a nation of Andy Hardys, and if, in a film, we see a frightened man wantonly take the life of another, it does not encourage us to do the same, any more than seeing an ivory hunter shoot an elephant makes us want to shoot one. It may, on the contrary, so sensitize us that we get a pang in the gut if we accidentally step on a moth.

> The accusation that the beauty of movie stars
> makes the anti-social acts of their characters
> dangerously attractive is . . . contrived.
> Actors and actresses are *usually* more
> beautiful than ordinary people . . . . Garbo's
> beauty notwithstanding, her "Anna
> Christie" did not turn us into whores, her
> "Mata Hari" did not turn us into spies, her
> "Anna Karenina" did not make us suicides.

There is always a lively discussion after I read these passages, each of which makes an important point about the purported effects of exposure to film violence. This, in turn, gives me a chance to discuss current research on her claims. Kael's analysis brings our discussion of media violence into contact with reality, with the actual film-going experience of individuals who are thought to be influenced one way or another by violent films. This contrasts with the artificial nature of most laboratory studies in this area. Regrettably, because they support the views of those who wish to regulate the media, they are the ones that are almost always cited in public policy discussions of this issue.

Every now and then, after mulling over a *New Yorker* essay, I will want to conduct a piece of research on a topic it has dealt with. This was certainly true in the case of Meghan Daum's article, "Virtual Love," which appeared in the August 25, 1997 issue, almost thirty years after Kael's review. Daum's essay, which the magazine placed in its "Brave New World Department," vividly recounts the reactions of a young woman to a romance that had originated on the Internet. It was not a happy experience, although when it began, Daum was instantly caught up in the "exhilaration" of digital courtship. She wrote:

> But, curiously, the Internet... felt anything but dehumanizing. My interaction with PFSlider seemed more authentic than much of what I experienced in the daylight realm of living beings. I was certainly putting more energy into the relationship than I had put into many others."

Her essay led me to wonder about the features of electronic communication that might facilitate the formation of online relationships and whether or not they differed from those established in the usual ways. I began by investigating the prevalence and durability of cyber-relationships. Daum reports that:

> ... at least seven people confessed to me the vagaries of their own E-mail affairs... This topic arose, unprompted, in the course of normal conversation.... we all shook our heads in bewilderment as we told our tales... These were normal people, writers and lawyers and scientists. They were all smart, attractive, and more than a little sheepish about admitting just how deeply they had been sucked in. Mostly, it was the courtship ritual that had seduced us. E-mail had become an electronic epistle, a yearned-for rule book. It allowed us to do what was necessary to experience love.

At the time, nothing was known about the frequency of cyber-romances. To find out, I surveyed over 1,000 students with Internet accounts at a nearby university and was surprised to learn that 36% of those who responded indicated they had formed a close friendship with another individual in an online setting. Twenty-two percent described it as a close romantic relationship. Even more surprising was the finding that, like Daum, the students did not characterize their online relationships as shallow or distant. Quite to the contrary, they claimed to have formed genuinely close friendships that were every bit as satisfying as those established in traditional ways. In fact, in some instances, they had led to marriage.

Most of the week, I do my research or I devote myself to teaching. In either case, the subject matter almost always has something to do with psychology, primarily social or environmental psychology. I am drawn by the relevance of these areas to everyday life. At times the research does capture my interest, occasionally it will even surprise me, but most of the time it does neither. Above all, it never fulfills a longing I seem to have for something of artistic or literary merit or that emotionally gives me pause.

More often than not, the *New Yorker* comes to my rescue. There I find the culture that is absent from my ordinary world and ideas that often seem truer than the ones I encounter in psychology. When I see the magazine in the mailbox, I must confess to being more than a little bit grateful that it has once again come my way. I welcome it like a close friend who stops by for a visit each week. The *New Yorker*, as Shawn put it, seems like "an oasis ... in a period in which so much of life is debased and corrupted.[6]" Yes, that is it, precisely.

I know my *New Yorker* is not everyone's *New Yorker.* But in reading the magazine each week, I have come to feel part of the community of other readers who value polished writing and serious commentary. The symbolic nature of this community makes it no less real. In *The World Through a Monocle,*[7] Mary Corey captured this bond quite well: "Some felt a profound kinship with the magazine because it spoke for them, giving a public voice to their own private intelligencies." It says "what I think and feel," a Washington, D.C. woman wrote, "as I should like to have said it."

In a sense, the *New Yorker* has become my "Third Place"—a term coined by Ray Oldenberg to refer to those informal gathering places in the community that an individual is drawn to each day outside of their home and workplace. French cafes, English pubs, and Italian piazzas are such places. I do not have a Third Place that I am drawn to at the end of the day. Indeed, I do not believe there are many such gathering places in this country.

However, at the *New Yorker,* I find a group of like-minded regulars who have come together for informal discussion and thoughtful banter and where someone can always be counted on for a good story or an idea worth considering. I go in solitude and while I can't converse with them, later, in other settings, I can speak with others about the "discussion" that I have overheard at the *New Yorker.*

While the regulars are different, to a certain extent, my experience resembles the one recounted by the main character in Erica Jong's novel, *Fear of Flying.*

It was not that I merely read the *New Yorker*,
I lived it in a private way. I had created for
myself a *New Yorker* world (located
somewhere east of Westport and west of the
Cotswolds) where Peter DeVries (punning
softly) was forever lifting a glass of
Piesporter, where Niccolo Tucci (in plum
velvet dinner jacket) flirted in Italian with
Muriel Spark, where Nabokov sipped tawny
port from a prismatic goblet (while a Red
Admirable perched on his pinky), and where
John Updike tripped over the master's Swiss
shoes, excusing himself charmingly
(repeating all the while that Nabokov was
the best writer of English currently holding
American citizenship).

This is the kind of special relationship that is said to
develop between the *New Yorker* and its readers and the
way in which the magazine has sustained and educated
me during all the years that I have been reading it.

One of the respondents to Ben Yagoda's[8] recent survey
of dedicated *New Yorker* readers recalled an experience
she had while serving as a nurse during World War II
in a remote section of northern Italy. She reported being
asked by a wounded soldier: "If you could have
anything right now, what would it be?" In an instant
she replied: "An issue of the *New Yorker* magazine."
Whereupon the two-wounded soldier, American nurse,
in that far-off time and place—began reminiscing about
their favorite *New Yorker* cartoons and writers. Deserted
island, northern Italian hospital, I can't imagine
responding any differently.

Notes

6   Cited in an unpublished paper, *We're Not Making For Automobiles! Writing, Reading and Professional Identity at the New Yorker*, presented by Trysh Travis at the Modern Language Association Meeting, 1996.

7   Mary F. Corey, *The World Through a Monocle: The New Yorker at Midcentury*. Cambridge: Harvard University Press, 1999.

8   Ben Yagoda, *About Town: The New Yorker and the World It Made*. New York: Scribner, 2000.

LETTER FROM FLORENCE

First of all it is necessary
to find yourself a country
—which is not easy.
It takes much looking
after which you must be lucky.

From *First of All*
Kenneth O. Hanson

Each year, as the winter drags on for what seems like forever, I make plans to visit Italy. I do not speak Italian and have little appreciation of its artistic treasures. I have no business or research to undertake here and I don't know anyone who lives in this country. It is enough to simply be in Italy, actually to be here in Florence where I spend most of my time, wandering through the narrow streets, listening to the people, astonished by their energy and the beauty that surrounds them.

Occasionally, I go out in the country or spend a few nights in a nearby hill town. I recall an excursion that I made last year. It began with a picnic in the village of Borgo Pretale, followed by an afternoon exploring Montepulcino, Montaclino and Monteriggioni. Those names! The heat, the light, the fields of oaks took me back to my youth in California. It is always like that. In the afternoon, I found myself lost on a back road somewhere in Tuscany. It was of no concern. Everything seemed quite familiar.

I feel at home here, even though I am in a hotel and hardly speak to anyone and then only about the most mundane matters. No one contacts me. My family is a continent away. Yet there is something about this place that puts me in touch with my roots. Florence feels like home, or more exactly, a place that I would be content to call my home, indeed, could have been my home, had my life taken a different course.

I know that the warmth of Italy draws me here as much as anything else, the warmth that begins at sunrise and lingers long into the night. That seems essential now and I know that I can count on it here, at least for a good part of the year. What is so important about the warmth? I wax and wane in thinking about this question. All I know is that here I am no longer plagued by dark and numb hands. I need not suit up to go outside, nor do I have to wear my hat all day, and wonder of wonders, it is even possible to dine alfresco much of the time.

I am also drawn by the pleasure of walking about this city. Normally, I go everywhere by car. Here, I go everywhere on foot, regardless of the distance. Never once have I taken a taxi or a bus in Florence. Never once have I ceased to be absorbed by my surroundings, as I saunter from one neighborhood to the next, most of which are not much different today than they were when the Medicis and Michelangelo ventured out. Those who live in Florence know this experience well:

Florentines and Tuscans have this innate
sense of taste that has remained during the
centuries. Walking through the city is like
walking through a fresco sometimes. It's as
if the faces of the artisans have remained the
same throughout the centuries. Their spirits
have remained as well.[9]

When I am in Florence or any of the Italian hill towns, I
begin to understand the meaning of a livable place. I
think about the mistakes that have been made in the
cities of my country and why most are so unlivable.
Where did we go wrong in America?

More than anything, I think it is the scale of things. You
see that clearly in Florence, where everything is so much
smaller than it is in America. The buildings are only a
few stories high at most and the shops are often not
much larger than a living room. Here, the streets are
narrow and irregular and it is sometimes difficult to
find a place to walk. To pass another person, you often
have to step off into the roadway, which can be
dangerous if the street is also wide enough to let cars
go zipping by, for that is the way they are driven here
in Italy.

Many of the buildings date from the Renaissance and
before. Some are beautiful palazzos or civic buildings,
meticulously preserved and thoroughly modernized
within. On every street, there are many small merchants,
each selling only a few items. The pattern is repeated
in the next block and on the next street over. Shops that
sell bread, fruit and vegetables, books, hardware, and
espresso are close by. I go from place to place, gathering
the things I need. Along the way, I try to exchange a

few words with the people I have come to "know"— that is, if they are not already chatting with someone else. I understand there are supermercatos on the outskirts of Florence, but you surely don't need them if you live within the city.

Many small craftsmen have their workshops in the heart of the neighborhood where they live. They know nothing of long commute trips on heavily congested roadways. The homes and shops of the carpenters, leatherworkers, bookbinders, painters, and metal craftsmen are surrounded by hotels, restaurants, and boutiques. There are no broad highways that cut across this Florence. No doubt, that has made an enormous difference. Although there are cars in this city, they are forbidden in many areas and are far outnumbered by the small motor scooters that are the primary mode of transport of the Florentines. Fortunately, this city, unlike those in our country, was designed for the people who live here, not for anything like an automobile.

In every neighborhood of Florence, there is a central square and, in some, many smaller ones. They vibrate with talk and music and the activity of the surrounding banks, restaurants, bookshops, churches, artisans, and whoever else is fortunate enough to be there. The piazza is the heart of any Italian town. It is the place to go and to be seen.

> Businessmen, farmers and students have a coffee and a croissant at the café on the square every morning, school-children gather to play soccer after school and a few hours later the whole town comes out for an

evening stroll. In a country where the houses are often built one right on top of another, and most towns were laid out in a time when the concept of urban space just didn't exist, the piazza is the setting for social life. This is even reflected in the expression in piazza, which literally means in public.[10]

Whatever happened to the public square in America? Whatever happened to the kind of experience that occurs each day in the piazza of every Italian village and town? There are few such gathering places in the USA, places that encourage an informal public life, where the spirit is playful and the purpose is socializing and the main activity is good conversation. I bemoan the absence of such places in my own country. Here, they are everywhere.

The sociability of the Italians is apparent the minute you set foot in this country. On the train from Milan to Florence, I sat next to two couples who were traveling together. Each pair sat facing the other. They were talking when I first sat down. They continued to talk until it was time to get off the train. All four participated in the jabber. Each one more animated than the other. Although I could not understand a word, it was a pleasure to listen to them. Compared to my silent world, theirs was a joy to behold.

Italians also love to stroll about their city. Much socializing is done this way. We may phone, or e-mail or meet a friend for lunch. Italians often get together by going for a walk. *La passeggiata*, the early-evening promenade that takes place in most Italian towns at the end of the working day, is a major social event, the Italian equivalent of our cocktail party. The tradition is said to be the strongest in the rural areas, where at the end of the day, most of the town folk amble up and down the main street, greeting and chatting with one another before eventually returning home for their evening meal.

It is not uncommon for Italians to walk arm-in-arm as they stroll down the avenue. Men with other men, women with other women, and mixed groups. There is nothing amorous about this; rather it is simply a reflection of the warmth of their relationship. Late one afternoon in Florence, I came upon a young Italian girl walking hand in hand with her father and then soon after, a young Italian boy walking together with his mother. Both children were engaged in a lively, carefree exchange with their parent. The experience came as a surprise, also with a twinge of envy.

These days, the men and women of Italy also spend a fair amount of time chatting on their cell phones. They carry on animated conversations on the streets, in restaurants, in hotel elevators—everywhere. On the train traveling from Zurich to Milan, a phone rang somewhere nearby. An elderly woman in the row ahead of mine opened her purse, took out her phone, and engaged in a lively conversation all the while we were winding our way down into Milan. I was entranced by the novelty of this scene. No one else took the slightest notice.

It is not surprising that Italians are so musical. It comes with the language. When Italians speak to one another, they virtually sing, with a rhythm and lyric that is slightly operatic. Soon the words echo in your mind, although you don't have the vaguest idea what they mean. I don't think it would be difficult to learn Italian. It was not long before I found myself quite unexpectedly speaking an Italian word or phrase that from all I could tell must have been appropriate. When most Italians talk, they also gesture vigorously with their hands, as if they were conducting an orchestra. I suspect that if you tied a rope around their hands, they would not be able to utter a single word.

During lunch one day at the Bar Pasticceria Curatone, I observed a riotous display of friendship and camaraderie. A middle-aged man, who was sitting by my table on the terrace, was engaged in a vigorous conversation with the bar's owner. Soon, some old friends happened by and when they saw him, each one, in turn, seemed to explode with shouts of joy and delight, followed by spirited conversation. In time, others passed by who also recognized one or more of the assembled group. Jumps for joy, long embraces, happy smiles, and long tales of "Where have you been? What have you been up to? How wonderful you look. Oh, let me show you the pictures of my baby." As if that wasn't enough, soon after that, I sat astonished as I observed a similar scene unfold at another table.

While I experience these encounters vicariously, they are no less pleasing. Actually, they are probably more so. All my pleasures here are solitary ones. Indeed, here I am, thrown back upon myself like nowhere else. There is no one I can understand. No one even tries to talk with me. The phone never rings. I am often asked if I mind being alone like this for so long. I always reply that I am never entirely alone in Florence. The city is too distracting; there is too much to see and hear. My days here are not the least bit solitary. Susan Jacoby put it well: "I have never spent an uninteresting day in this city, never experienced small vicissitudes or deeper sorrows that could not be ameliorated by contact with the noble civilization of these stony streets."[11]

Yet Florentines don't spend all their time socializing. One night at a trattoria in a residential district quite far from the city center, I was one of a group of 5 men who were seated alone for dinner. Two were laborers who had come in after a hard day of moving rocks or steel. Another was a white-collar worker and then a casual, but well-dressed, man of clearly refined taste. I was reading my book, another his newspaper, and three others were staring into space. Another night, I watched a man punching buttons on a storefront machine in a residential area of Florence. It was an automatic video vender that operates like a cash machine. He inserted his card, read the menu of available videos, requested a brief review of those he was interested in, selected the one he wanted, and hit the button. Bingo, it came rolling out the slot. All the videos were visible behind the window of this unattended mini-store. No human intervention. No exchange of cash. No talk or banter about the films. Just the person, the card, and those buttons.

Nothing is perfect or so I have been told. So I must confess then that the noise on the streets of Florence and elsewhere in Italy can be annoying. On the streets, it comes primarily from the roar of the Vespas. But there is also the horrible music that is played in many places now—restaurants, bars, on the rooftop terrace, and down in the lobby. And each morning as I look out over the piazza, I am dismayed to see the litter (paper, containers, soda pop cans) that is strewn everywhere.

Such a lovely square marred by all that carelessness, that total disregard for the public space. Eventually, the men come with their sweeper and bags to clean it up. The mini-streetcleaner follows, to do the same for the pavement. Then, in the last of the morning light, the square looks quite lovely. But as the day goes by, the litter begins to accumulate, the crowds increase and by the end of the evening, once more the litter is everywhere. There are collection containers placed throughout the piazza. I am annoyed they are not more widely used. What is the great pleasure of throwing your rubbish on the grass?

It was hot and sultry on my last Sunday in Florence. The streets were quiet, the mood subdued, and the usually bustling city became a sleepy hillside village in the molten hot air. And so I went to the Cascine, the enormous park at the south end of Florence that stretches for miles along the Arno. I wanted to take some pictures, Sunday in the Park, Sunday in the Cascine. But it was impossible. I could not intrude upon these people. The old man playing his harmonica, the lovers on the grass, the young boys playing soccer, and the rollerbladers taking their spills. I walked deep into the park that day and I have many lasting impressions, but none of them are on film.

A light rain fell in Florence the night before I left so the air was clear on my early- morning walk. Although I had passed by many times before, the buildings seemed so different in the half-dark of that time of day. Still I continued to take it all in. I thought it must be like a child's view of the world, echoing Doris Lessing's impressions of London, after arriving from Rhodesia, which I was reading at the time:

> I was returned to a child's way of seeing and
> feeling, every person, building, bus, street
> striking my senses with the shocking
> immediacy of a child's life, everything
> oversized, very bright, very dark, smelly,
> noisy. I do not experience London like that
> now.[12]

I reached the station only a few moments before the
train to Milan was scheduled to leave and so I jumped
aboard the first car at the platform. It turned out to be
the last car of a very long train. When we arrived in
Milan, the car I was on did not reach the station platform
area. To get off, you had to leap from the car's steps all
the way down to the gravel bed. It was quite a distance
from that last step to the gravel bed. I jumped off first
with suitcase in hand. An old lady, perhaps from Sicily,
wearing that marvelous Sicilian black, followed me in
turn. I thought I better stay to help her. She was clearly
not an expert jumper.

As I was guiding her down the last step, she came
tumbling down upon me. In turn, I fell back and thought,
well, this is surely it. I could hear the bones cracking
against the tracks and the siren of the ambulance off in
the distance. It was horrible, the old lady falling off the
step as I was heading directly for those shiny steel
tracks. I was terribly bruised. The old lady just muttered
something and walked away. No *scusas*. No one stopped
to inquire how I was. All I could do was whisper an
obscenity and hobble off to the airport bus.

I know Florence can never be my home. It is too late
for that now. I wrack my brains to think of a place in
America where I can live as I do when I am here. I am

doing much "looking" for one now. Here I see gaiety and friendship and community. I need only glance out the window or sit in a piazza. Smiles and shouting and good cheer everywhere. Sun and warmth throughout the day and night and more of the same tomorrow. Even if I am only a visitor, Florence brings me closer to the place I am searching for now, closer to much that is also absent from my life. Is it any wonder I keep coming back?

Notes

9   Contessa Simonetta Brandolini d'Adda. *Robb Report*, April 2000.

10   *Vista Magazine.* Essay on the Italian Piazza. Summer 2000.

11   *New York Times* Learning to Live with Arrivederci. October 12, 1997

12   Roads to London, *Granta* 58: Ambition, Summer 1997.

EXCHANGES

Poetry not as way of depicting the world but as a way of conversing with it, trying to know it. But knowing is not easy . . . . You start out with a blank piece of paper. But it starts turning into silence, and the silence feels like it's in conversation with you. The silence comes in and says, "But how about this?" And I don't believe what you're saying. And it goes, "uh-uh. Try again."

Jorre Graham

WHATEVER HAPPENED TO LETTER WRITING?

Letter writing is not the noble enterprise. Remaining fully expressive is the noble enterprise.

Vivian Gornick

The other day, I received a gift from a friend. Naturally, I wanted to thank him. I thought of phoning, but he lived out of town and was probably at work anyway. Besides, the gift deserved more than a phone call. I could have e-mailed, but he is not yet with-it digitally. Or I could have written a letter.

To phone, e-mail or write? That, in a nutshell, is the gist of a modern communication dilemma. I like to do all three. Sometimes one, sometimes another. But I write letters far less often than I wish I did or than I used to.

Fifty years ago, people wrote letters. I was in grammar school then and each summer when I went to camp, I was asked to send a postcard home every day. I recall protesting, not so much because I didn't like to write, but because I couldn't imagine having anything new to say each day. "Well, tell us what you had to eat," I was told in reply.

I continued to send a letter home at least once a week throughout my college days and for many years thereafter until there was no longer anyone left to write to. In those days, we didn't telephone as much. It seemed expensive. And no one had ever heard of an e-mail or a fax.

All the letters I ever wrote home were saved. The little cards from camp, the letters I wrote whenever I was traveling, and all of those I wrote as I grew older. At the end of each year, my mother tied them together with a large rubber band and put them in the trunk I had taken to camp each summer at the start of my letter-writing days. When she died, I didn't know what to do with that trunk packed full of my letters. I thought: this is ridiculous, no one, not even I, will ever be the least bit interested in reading them again. So I threw them all away.

The days of writing letters are over now. Very few individuals write them any more. Yet, I still like to write. I write to my children. They never reply. That doesn't deter me. Sometimes we have a problem or disagree about something. So I write to explain myself. But I have learned that writing a letter about the matter never works. Yet when we speak on the telephone, it rarely takes more than a few moments to work things out.

In the introduction to *The Oxford Book of Letters*, the editors, Frank and Anita Kermode[13], make the following claim: "Most of us write at least half a dozen letters of one sort or another every week, so that in the fifty or sixty years of a normal letter-writing life many people must dispatch 18,000 letters." Am I reading that correctly? Who in the world could they be talking about? Since they are English, they are no doubt referring to people who live in Great Britain. But it is hard to imagine the British are much different in this respect than individuals who live in the United States. I suspect most of us are lucky if we write half a dozen genuine letters in a year.

As I thought about all this a while ago, I was led to wonder about the letter-writing experience of other individuals. How often do they write a personal letter to someone else? Is it as infrequent as I suspect or closer to the Kermode's weekly estimate of at least half a dozen?

To find out, I conducted an informal survey of students at the Northwestern School of Law in Portland, Oregon. I chose this group because I wanted a sample of well-educated individuals, who varied in terms of age, income, and occupational status.[14] Students in four different classes received the survey during the first week of the 1997 academic year. Of the 125 that were distributed, 112 were returned—an unusually high rate.

In the survey I asked the students if they had written a personal letter that day. Ninety-one percent said they had not, while 9% said they had. I also asked them to estimate the number of letters they wrote each week. Almost half (47.3%) reported they never did, while 38% said they were lucky if they wrote once a week. The remaining individuals estimated they wrote between two and five letters per week.

I also asked the students to indicate their preferred method of communicating with someone else. Relative to the telephone and e-mail, letter writing was the least preferred. Only 4% said it was their first choice, while the telephone was ranked number one by 47% of the sample, followed, in turn, by e-mail (34%). The remaining 15% said they couldn't decide between the telephone and e-mail.

In a word, this well-educated group of individuals confirmed what many have come to bemoan. People have more or less stopped writing letters and those who still do constitute a relatively small minority. However, even they don't write very often. When we asked the students why they didn't write letters any more, the majority (65%) said it was simply a matter of not having enough time. Others mentioned they were simply too busy (4%), too lazy (4%) or just didn't like to write letters (5%).

In a deeply felt lament of this situation, the author Vivian Gornick[15] reflects on the pressures that get in the way of writing letters.

> A few days later I had to deliver a piece of information to a friend who lives in SoHo, one ZIP code away from my apartment. I reached for the phone, then stopped, my hand hovering over the receiver. I did not, at that moment, want to talk to my friend. Yet I wanted to speak to her. Suddenly, I wanted to write a letter. I wanted to tell my friend on paper how the information had come into my hands, what I had thought when I'd received it, what I was thinking now. I wanted to describe the light in my

room as I was writing, the air as it felt when I came home, an exchange I had just had in the elevator. I wanted to narrate, not to transmit: to enlarge on the moment, impose shape: achieve forms. It would be a different piece of information my friend would then receive, coming through the mail rather than over the phone . . . . No sooner did I sit down at the computer than the impulse began to fragment. I was tired. I was going out again in two hours. Did I have enough time to write this? I consulted the groove in my brain for letter-writing sentences. It felt stiff and narrow. So long since I'd written a letter! Maybe tomorrow. Then I remembered that my friend needed the information within two days. If I wrote, she might have my letter the day after tomorrow; then again, she might have it in a week. I could not rely on mail delivery. What the hell, I thought, take a chance. I turned on the computer. God, I was tired! I turned off the machine and picked up the phone.

Is the situation as bleak as Gornick implies? Has letter writing fallen victim to fatigue, convenience, and the lure of instant communication? Gornick wrote her essay in 1994, before the explosive growth of electronic communication. So it is not surprising that she viewed the telephone as the primary enemy of letter writing. But much has changed since then. Within this short span of time, the world of letter writing has been transformed by the Internet. Individuals now dispatch countless letter-looking documents that, taken together, must run into the millions each day.

After we administered our survey, several students told us they thought letter writing was making a comeback because of e-mail. They reported they never used to write letters, but now that they have Internet accounts, they are much more likely to write to their friends and family than they used to. And much of what they write consists of letters or messages that bear a striking resemblance in both form and content to a traditional letter. Before the Internet, individuals may have written letters or postcards. Perhaps now they write the same messages and send them over the Internet.

Several commentators have taken issue with this claim, arguing that electronic epistles bear only a distant relationship with traditional letters. Oxenhandler[16] maintains they differ greatly in their *temporal features*, in the rhythms associated with how each is composed and sent. She writes:

> . . . . I used to love the feeling of dropping a letter into the box. For several days, the letter-in-transit would hover around the edges of my consciousness. This delay was an intrinsic part of the pleasure of letter writing. It had a special tense all its own: when the "must do" turns into the "just done." And, as the letter hovered, I also savored a kind of prescience in relation to my friend. During those two or three days, I knew, at least in some small measure, what would befall her: *a letter in the box!* As Iris Murdoch has written, "The sending of a letter constitutes a magical grasp upon the future." But now the old magic has given way to the new. And though a fax or an e-mail may lie in wait for

its recipient, it nonetheless gets from here to there in a matter of moments, and its waiting has none of the sealed mystery about it that attends a letter in its envelope.

Others have pointed out that letters have a degree of *permanence* that is quite different from messages sent over the Internet. In a review of M. F. K. Fischer's *A Life in Letters*, Fussell[17] comments: "Had she lived in another decade, many of her letters might have been lost forever, flashed on screen to be read and discarded in a matter of minutes. *A Life in Letters* reminds one of what is lost in the magic of electronic mail: permanence."

Others maintain that letter writing is a more *literate* form of communication than e-mailing—". . . letter writing was a noble enterprise that went uninterrupted until our own day, when technology has all but killed off the form." (John Bayley as quoted by Gornick) And the Kermodes admit that while it may be an advantage to transmit the written word instantly, they find it impossible to imagine that there will ever be "an Oxford Book of E-mail."

I believe the authors of these critiques have prematurely concluded that letter writing has succumbed to the Internet. Sending an e-mail without much deliberation is by no means a universal practice. And it is surely not characteristic of messages composed off-line or until the author has time to reply. I often write messages off-line, especially when I want them to be well written. They are not composed in a frenzy or carelessly edited. Indeed, I write them with as much thought and reflection as I used to take, long before the Internet was even imagined.

A student recently wrote that she does much the same. She told me about a close relationship she had established with a "gentleman," as she put it, who lived in a distant state. It cost too much for them to telephone one another each day. So for economic reasons their correspondence was carried out primarily through e-mail. She wrote: "I can assure you that I spent ample time crafting those expressions, equal to if not greater than most of my paper letters."

The recipient may take just as much time and care in replying, so that the entire exchange may take several days or weeks to complete. In this way, an online exchange can mirror the delicate temporal features of sending and receiving a letter through the mail. The correspondence can give rise to most of the pleasures Oxhenhandler believes to be true of the traditional letter-writing experience. The author can mull over what he or she has written, savor the period between the transmission of the message and its receipt, and take pleasure in imagining the reader's response. In turn, the process can be repeated by the recipient in composing a reply and anticipating its receipt.

E-mail messages can also be every bit as tangible and as permanent as a valued held-in-the-hand letter which is read over and over again. They can be saved in files or printed so that they are physically indistinguishable from a traditional letter. My student also confirmed this in her message by adding: "I also printed and kept every correspondence so that in fact I do have a paper trail of that period."

In short, e-mail messages do not simply disappear after they have been sent. Nor must they be replied to instantly. And there is nothing about e-mail messages *per se* that prevents them from being every bit as literate or poetic as traditional letters. Thus, I find wanting the claim that communicating on the Internet is any less "noble" than letter writing. All of the skills that go into composing intelligent letters can be readily applied in that setting.

Moreover, like so many others, I find writing e-mails far less effortful than penning them to paper. In typing a message on the keyboard my thoughts seem to fly right out onto the screen, whereas when I try to write them on stationery, a fair number are lost in the process. Like the students in my study, Gornick speaks of letter writing as a "chore," as "tiresome." There is little doubt about it— by contrast, writing letters on the computer is a breeze.

Is it too easy? Do we write e-mails when we *should* be writing traditional letters instead? I grappled with this problem recently in writing to the parents of the woman that my son recently became engaged to marry. I wanted to tell them how happy I was that he had, at long last, found someone who meant as much to him as she did. I wanted to tell them how much I admired their daughter. I wanted to try to arrange to meet them before the wedding.

I spent a good deal of time crafting this letter. Naturally, this was done on the computer. When I had finished, I puzzled over how to send it. Should I print the letter, put it in an envelope, and post it in the mail? Or simply e-mail it to them? Yes, the posted letter still seemed the proper thing to do and I didn't want them to think I didn't know my manners.

But I wanted to communicate with them right away. I knew the letter would take the better part of a week to reach them. What would be so wrong about e-mailing it to them? In either case, the message would be identical. I thought about situations that definitely call for a traditional letter. A condolence must surely be one. And yet I recalled that when my brother passed away a short time ago, I received at least a dozen e-mail condolences written by individuals from whom I had not heard in years.

I was not the least bit offended that they wrote me this way. In fact, most were old friends from whom I was delighted to hear. Following their initial message, we engaged in a lively e-mail exchange for a short time after. So in this case, the Internet made it possible for us to reestablish a relationship that had all but vanished, even though it was occasioned by a situation that might have more "properly" been initiated by a formal letter. However, in all likelihood, the letter never would have been written in the first place.

"Get with it, Richard," I declared. I e-mailed the parents my letter. They replied in kind the very next day. We have been e-mailing each other with pleasure ever since. Thank God for the Internet!

It is situations like this that explains why the Internet has restored the practice of letter writing to so many individuals. It has not, thereby, fostered a renaissance in eloquence, but the medium doesn't preclude it any more than it precludes well-crafted sentences, smart editing or thoughtful revising. Taking the long view, I suspect that the Internet has given rise to new styles of writing that will eventually establish their own, quite respectable, place in literary history. So perhaps the Kermodes are right after all. Over the course of a lifetime, many of us do write several thousand letters. Only now we deliver them over the Internet rather than through the postal service.

Notes

13   Kermode, F. & Kermode, A. (Eds.) Introduction to *The Oxford Book of Letters*. 1995. Oxford University Press: Oxford.

14   There were slightly more females (55%) than males (45%) in the sample whose members ranged in age from 19 to 60 years with an overall mean of 29 years. Although the majority (80%) listed student as their current occupation, they differed widely in the previous jobs they had held. Approximately 40% reported they had been employed by accounting concerns, 12% by law firms, while the remaining listed a variety of other professions.

15   Gornick, Vivian. Letters are acts of faith; telephone calls are a reflex. *New York Times*. July 31, 1994.

16   Oxenhandler, Noelle. Fall from Grace. *New Yorker*, June 16, 1997.

17   Fussell, Betty. Calculated Seduction: M.F.K. Fisher A Life in Letters Correspondence 1929-1991 *New York Times Book Review*, January 18, 1998

ON WRITING THERAPY

Words can kill: this we know only too well. But words can, in small measure, also sometimes heal.

Amos Oz

Writing is a form of therapy; sometimes I wonder how all those who do not write, compose or paint can manage to escape the madness, the melancholia, the panic fear which is inherent in the human condition.

Graham Greene

I went to my first writer's workshop last summer. It was in Italy. Maybe I would not have gone had it been elsewhere. However, a writer whom I have admired and respected for years was teaching a class on the essay and the memoir. While I can scarcely claim to be a "writer," recently I have been trying to write personal essays and I knew that I would learn a great deal from her class.

My hope was amply confirmed, as she was every bit as instructive in person as she is on the written page.

Initially I was worried that my lack of writing background would prove to be embarrassing. I found, to the contrary, that I could hold my own with her, as well as the other students in the class, many of whom had also been writing professionally for years.

The workshop was held in Assisi, a much-visited hill town in southern Umbria. I treasured every moment. I loved being in Italy—the warmth, the crazy, wonderful people, the food, the endless days and nights of utter pleasure. My room looked out over fields of sunflowers and the steep, winding streets of Assisi. As I was sitting at my desk, the town below and all of Umbria lay before me.

There were ten of us in the class that met every day but one for two consecutive weeks. Each of us presented something we had written before coming to the workshop. We were not asked to do any new writing, although I know many of the students wrote a great deal while they were there.

I asked the class to read an essay that I had written about my lifelong devotion to the *New Yorker* magazine. The other members of the class, all of whom were women, presented memoirs that were deeply charged tales of personal conflict, marital strife, difficult mother-daughter relationships, sibling rivalry, unruly children, or a shattered love affair. I was struck by the sameness of their accounts, by the sadness that ran through them all. I kept thinking there surely must be more to writing memoirs than page after page of emotional turmoil. Yet, other than my own essay, no one wrote about anything other than a failed relationship.

I thought a lot about why the students were so preoccupied with their cheerless experiences. Their accounts reminded me of James Pennebaker's recent book, *Opening Up: The Healing Power of Expressing Emotions*, which reviews recent research on the therapeutic effects of writing about emotional experiences.[18] Reading about the psychological and physiological studies in Pennebaker's book had been an eye-opening experience for me, as it was my first exposure to writing therapy. In recalling Pennebaker's research, I began to view the student's memoirs as largely therapeutic, that, like the subjects in his studies, they were also trying to alleviate their emotional distress by writing about their misfortunes. Since Pennebaker's book seemed so closely associated with the students' memoirs, I decided to summarize it for them during one of our last classes.

My review must have struck a responsive chord as it elicited a lively discussion during and after class. The students recognized that individuals can obtain some degree of relief by *talking* about their distress in a therapeutic setting, but they were not aware that simply *writing* about it could also be therapeutic. In his book, Pennebaker marshals an impressive array of evidence to show that writing about emotional experiences has the same positive effects on physical and mental heath as discussing them with a trained therapist.

In an early study, for example, he employed two groups of individuals. Those in one group were asked to write about extremely important emotional issues, while those in the other group wrote about neutral topics. The individuals in both groups wrote for 15 to 30 minutes each day for 3 to 5 days. They usually wrote in the laboratory and were never given any feedback about their written material.

Pennebaker says: "The degree to which writing or talking about basic thoughts and feelings can produce such profound physical and psychological changes is nothing short of amazing." He reports that it leads to fewer illnesses and physician visits, improvements in immune function and decreasing stress as measured by autonomic function. Students show an improvement in their grade point average. Employees report a decline in work absenteeism and an increased likelihood of reemployment following job loss. And the majority of research participants indicate they experience less stress, negative affect, and symptoms of depression.

In another study, Pennebaker reports that the spouses of individuals who committed suicide reported having fewer health problems when they spoke to others about this traumatic event than those who did not. Indeed, spouses who did not talk about their partner's death experienced higher levels of anxiety, depression, and insomnia.

According to Pennebaker, suppressing the expression of upsetting events is harmful and over a period of time becomes a serious health risk. In contrast, facing them squarely by talking and writing about them has the opposite effect. How does writing accomplish this? In trying to answer this question, Pennebaker reflects on his own experiences:

> In writing about upsetting events, for example, I often came to a new understanding of the emotional events

themselves. Problems that had seemed overwhelming became more circumscribed and manageable after I saw them on paper. In some way, writing about my haunting experiences helped to resolve them. Once the issues were resolved, I no longer thought about them.

Pennebaker suggests that writing therapy is not unlike the Zeigarnick effect, a phenomenon observed in the study of memory. This effect refers to the fact that *interrupted* tasks tend to be more accurately recalled than completed ones. For example, individuals prevented from completing a story will be more likely to recall it accurately, and for a longer period of time, than they would if they had finished it. In like fashion, writing about a troubling experience enables the author to give some closure to it, perhaps to resolve it and thereby put it aside, instead of ruminating about it day after day.

Writing provides an occasion to work through events in a more logical fashion. It externalizes a traumatic experience, gets it out into the world, so to speak, so that it can be viewed in a different light. Pennebaker also suggests that self-disclosure, the act of telling others about significant personal experiences, accounts for a substantial portion of the therapeutic effects of writing. In this sense, writing is not unlike psychotherapy. In that situation, you speak to a trained professional about significant personal events, whereas when you write about them, you may be expressing the same things privately. Pennebaker also points out that writing about emotional experiences mimics, to a certain extent, the circumstances under which confession occurs in religious settings.

Is writing about upsetting events as effective as talking about them with a therapist? While not directly addressed by Pennebaker, Donnelly and Murray (1991) have recently examined this question.[19] They report that when there are at least four sessions, the changes produced by writing are indistinguishable from those produced by traditional therapy.

Recently, I have also begun to wonder if writing e-mails to another person about emotional experiences might also have therapeutic effects. The written word of e-mail is not unlike other forms of writing and the interactive nature of this type of exchange has much in common with a psychotherapeutic exchange. I recall an e-mail my wife sent me a few years ago, when we were living and working in different cities. While we spoke daily on the telephone, we also communicated a good deal by e-mail. One night during a stressful time for her, she e-mailed me: "It's 1 am. X says I shouldn't write you in the wee hours of the morning, that depression is at its height then and nothing seems possible. But I am doing it anyway. *Somehow I find it cathartic. I always feel better after putting my thoughts down.*" [Italics mine]

Communicating online like this has all the markings of writing therapy. Individuals find it consoling to e-mail someone about their emotional distress. Sometimes it might even be a person they haven't met. I wonder if the effects Pennebaker reports in *Opening Up* would also be true for exchanging e-mail messages with another person on the Internet? Would a group of individuals who are e-mailing about stressful matters be more likely to show the kinds of benefits he describes than a group e-mailing about neutral matters?

At the present time there is no evidence on this question. But it leads me to wonder if part of the attraction of online communication stems from the way it gives individuals an opportunity to write about emotional experiences that are normally suppressed. Indeed, perhaps e-mailing is another way to initiate and maintain the process of healing produced by writing or speaking to someone about those experiences.

Under certain conditions anonymous online disclosures might even be more effective than those expressed in a therapeutic situation. In a recent discussion of online communication, Gwinell (1998) notes that:

> People generally compose e-mail, however, in relationship to the written word, alone with their computer. The sense of the person to whom the e-mail will later be sent is not immediate, the way the presence of a living person is. Being alone with one's thoughts also opens the way for thoughts to arise that would be very difficult to express to another human being present in the room.[20]

It all sounds so simple. We all write. Some of us write in our journals or we write letters and now e-mails. We all are doing battle with one thing or another. The research on writing therapy tells us that to win our battles we need only spend a little time each day writing about them.

Can it be this simple? Were that it was so. There is much to be skeptical about in the many studies of writing therapy. We know, for example, that not every study reports a positive outcome. In those that do, we know that not all individuals have benefited from the writing experience. Nor do we know how long the positive effects last or if another group of individuals who did not write about their emotional experiences would show comparable changes during the same period of time. Above all, we do not know the mechanism responsible for the observed results. Pennebaker has proposed several—disinhibition, self-disclosure, and insight. But these alternatives are not clearly distinguished from one another and there are few, if any, reported tests designed to choose between them.

In *Opening Up,* Pennebaker reports an interesting finding. Across four days of writing, individuals who wrote *less* benefited more than did those who wrote the most about their distress. This indicates that something other than simply writing about emotional experiences is responsible for the positive effects of writing therapy. In analyzing the content of the writing samples, Pennebaker found that those whose physical and mental health improved the most tended to use more *causal analysis* [italics mine]. This finding is supported by a recent study demonstrating that expressive writing is likely to have the greatest benefits when it has a narrative structure.[21] Individuals who wrote tales that consisted largely of fragmented memories did not benefit as much as those who had organized them into a coherent narrative.

This line of research is consistent will all that I learned at the summer writing workshop. There we were taught that simply writing without a narrative structure, without an "organizing principle," is not literature. It appears that it is also not an effective form of writing therapy. For both to work there has to be a larger theme, a "revelation," as our teacher put it. At the workshop, we were taught that a narrative of personal feelings does not constitute literature. The author of a personal memoir has an obligation to come to a larger understanding of their experience, rather than simply recounting it, one incident after another, no matter how moving or eloquent.

I am not sure any of the memoirs presented at the workshop reached this kind of self-understanding. While writing them may have been temporarily therapeutic, most of us who were readers found them wanting in terms of psychological or literary wisdom. Many journeys were recounted, but few, if any, became tales of self-discovery.

I believe we are deluding ourselves by thinking we can put our emotional problems behind us simply by writing about them. Long ago, we learned to be skeptical of the claims of the "insight" theory of psychotherapy. Awareness is not sufficient to cure. Similarly, the evidence on writing therapy suggests considerable caution about accepting its various claims of success.

Long before I ever heard of "writing therapy," I wrote in my journal. I know that I am much more likely to write when things are not going well. But I also know that no matter how much I write or how much truth there is in what I write, I do not thereby put the problems behind me. I may feel a little better after I compose the passages. But only for the moment. Eventually the problems disappear. However, I realize full well that this occurs for reasons that have very little, if anything, to do with the fact that I may have written about them.

Notes

18   Pennebaker, J. (1997). *Opening Up: The Healing Power of Expressing Emotions*. New York: The Guilford Press.

19   Donnelly, D.A. & Murray, E.J. (1991). Cognitive and emotional changes in written essays and therapy interviews. *Journal of Social and Clinical Psychology*, 10, 334-350.

20   Gwinell, E. (1998). *Online Seduction: Falling in Love with Strangers on the Internet*. New York: Kodansha International.

21   Smyth, J., True, N., & Souto, J. (2001). Effects of writing about traumatic experiences: The necessity for narrative structuring. *Journal of Social and Clinical Psychology*, 20, 161-172.

DIGITAL PING-PONG

*Ah, this legendary ability of words to imply
more than reality can provide.*

Joseph Brodsky

For days now, my e-mail server has been "down" or
operating only intermittently. There are long periods
when it is impossible to send or receive messages. At other
times, the messages drift in a day or two after they were
sent. Nothing can be done about it. I am annoyed. I am
even more isolated, more cut-off than usual and have
come to realize how much I depend on e-mail now or to
put it more exactly, how much I need it.

E-mail has become my preferred means of
communication. There is no one to telephone. No one
telephones me. There is no reason to see anyone now.
The Internet is all that is left. Actually, I am no better off
there. Who is there to send an e-mail to? Even when I
send one, only rarely do I receive a reply and if one is,
by chance, sent now, I will probably never get it or it
will arrive days later, when it is no longer of much use
anyway.

However, none of this matters that much. What really
matters is the pleasure of *writing* the message. I seem

to have developed a zest for writing e-mails. There are times when I would like to emerge from my cave to talk with someone. And I seem to be at my best and most at ease communicating online, rather than in person. My condition is not unlike Wendy Lesser's who, soon after setting up her e-mail account, wrote:

> I became an e-mail maniac, checking in every hour or so and collapsing with disappointment if I got the empty-mailbox beep. I found myself waxing expansive onscreen, chatting on about virtually nothing. I was responding, I now think, to the special enticements of the form's mixed nature—at once private and public, solitary and communal, so that it seems to combine the two oldest types of American writing, the diary and the sermon.[22]

I am aware of the differences between communicating online, in person or on the telephone and it is fairly clear why e-mail has this effect. In cyberspace, I am anonymous, no one sees me, I do not see them, I am alone and am completely immune from the pressures that exist when other people are present. On the Internet, I can be myself without fear of judgment or evaluation. And so I am more open, I can speak more honestly, more readily, and with greater intimacy. It no longer surprises me that I and so many others can appear ever so much more eloquent online than in person or even on the phone.

In an interview in the *New York Times* about her novel *Virtual Love*, written in the form of e-mail dialogue between two lovers, the psychiatrist Avodah Offit captured the fundamental power of this situation:

> I think this whole E-mail revolution fulfills real needs, the human needs for intimacy and creativity. For thousands of years, people have been developing their literacy, but there have been very few outlets for most people. People were starved. They could not express themselves easily, as they can with E-mail, or get the kind of immediate reaction that you can electronically. That's why E-mail is so popular. It's a whole creative urge that is being satisfied.

The distinctive quality of e-mail talk also contributes to this effect. An e-mail is not altogether like writing or speaking. Rather, it seems more like a third form of communication, independent of either but combining elements of both. Its hybrid nature seems to have spawned a new medium, one that is adaptable to a variety of purposes, from the informal to the serious. It has also given rise to a richly inventive use of language. I often find myself saying things in an e-mail that I've never said or even thought about before.

For many individuals, e-mail has also become a place to socialize. The Internet is far more than a source for finding and manipulating information. It is also a *social technology,* one that allows individuals to establish new relationships and sustain old ones, sometimes with greater depth than was possible before and certainly with greater ease in the case of those separated by large distances.

Every once in a while, I have an e-mail buddy. The relationship has always started with great promise and has always ended badly. My first e-mail buddy was a student from one of my classes, a woman about the same age as my children no less. Our electronic correspondence lasted far too long and its effects were far from salutary.

One day, a woman in Canada sent me an e-mail expressing interest in my research. We started to exchange e-mails. Soon they became more personal. She was clever, witty, and funny. The frequency of our exchanges increased. She said she wanted to meet me. I told her to invite me to her town to consult about the work I was doing. She did. I went. It was a disaster.

All the fun and joy we had in e-mailing disappeared almost the moment we met. The reality was nothing like the make-believe. She was no longer the clever, witty or funny person she was online. I am sure she felt the same about me. I left the next day. Afterwards, she sent one more e-mail. She said she had been charmed by my words, that it was my words that she had fallen for, but the real me was not the least bit lovable.

In retrospect, I am sure none of these relationships would have developed were it not for electronic mail. The simple act of writing messages back and forth was their driving force. The exchange was exciting. It gave each of us a chance to tell our stories, to string together words as cleverly as possible and the immense pleasure of finding someone who seemed to listen and even be amused by it all. In another context, Vivian Gornick described what is at work in this situation:

> Nothing makes me feel more alive, and in
> the world, than the sound of my own mind
> working the presence of one that's
> responsive.[23]

Others have written about their online experiences in much the same way. No one has done this with more insight than Megham Daum in her *New Yorker* essay, *Virtual Love*.[24] While Daum describes her experience in an informal and candid fashion, I have derived from it six very general features of electronic communication that explains why it can so readily give rise to an online relationship. Each is illustrated with a passage from her tale.

1. Online communication liberates individuals from social anxiety.

    > *"But I have a constant low-grade fear of the telephone, and I often call people with the intention of getting their answering machines. There is something about the live voice that I have come to find unnervingly organic, as volatile as live television. E-mail provides a useful antidote for my particular communication anxieties."*

2. E-mail dialogues foster self-disclosure and personal intimacy.

    > *"I had previously considered cyber-communication an oxymoron, a fast road to the breakdown of humanity. But curiously, the Internet—at least in the limited form in which I was using it—felt anything but dehumanizing.*

> *My interaction with X seemed more authentic than much of what I experienced in the daylight realm of living beings. I [teased] him in a way I would never have dared to do in person, or even on the phone."*

3. E-mail encourages flirting and coquetry.

> *"I revealed very little about myself, relying instead on the ironic commentary and forced witticisms that are the conceit of so many E-mail messages . . . For me, the time online with X was far superior to the phone . . . I [teased] him in a way I would never have dared to in person, or even on the phone."*

4. Individuals construct elaborate fantasies of others when they are not present.

> *". . . though we both knew that the 'me' in his mind consisted largely of himself . . . I was horrified by the realization that I had invested so heavily in a made-up character—a character in whose creation I'd had a greater hand than even X himself . . . . X was more a concept than a person."*

5. An online personality can be quite unlike the real one.

> *"He stood before me, all flesh and preoccupation, and for this I could not forgive him . . . . The physical world had invaded our space . . . . X has known how to get me where I lived until he came to where I lived: then he became as unmysterious as anyone next door."*

6. Online relationships are intensified by the absence of physical proximity.

> *"Our need to worship somehow fuses with our need to be worshipped. It upsets me still further to see how inaccessibility can make this entanglement so much more intoxicating."*

What a terrific new world the Internet has created. We are doing nothing more than sitting at our desk, peering at our computer screen, and madly typing messages to another person. Magically we are transformed by this situation into the person we had always hoped to be but could never quite pull off. Freed from all that normally constrains us, we are no longer anxious. We are at ease speaking publicly about what is usually private. We say things we could never imagine uttering elsewhere. We flirt in a way we can never bring ourselves to do in the real world. The language flows. And we do all this with an individual we cannot see, indeed, may never have even met, and who, as a result, is largely a mirage.

The situation may be terrific, but it can also be a trap. It is easy to be snared by everything that is concealed in an e-mail dialogue. Individuals are faceless, they are voiceless, there is no way to detect their expressive behaviors, body language or any of the subtle signals we normally rely upon to detect the meaning of their words. More often than not, this terrific new world comes crashing down upon us when we finally come face to face with the person we have been volleying back and forth with all this time. Daum admits:

> If Pete and I had met at a party, we probably wouldn't have spoken to each

other for more than ten minutes, and that would have made life easier but also less interesting.

But they did meet online and, however brief it was, they did have an exhilarating long-distance courtship. Online, they seemed as alluring as anyone they had ever fallen for before. In person, they were little more than an unappealing date.

From all accounts, Daum's online encounter is not uncommon, although not everyone reports such a disappointing outcome. With increasing frequency, individuals say they have developed satisfying long-term relationships, including marriage, with a person they have met online. I recall a message a student sent me after we had discussed online relationships in class one day.

> My father-in-law, who was married to the same woman for 30 years, met someone on a Prodigy Bulletin Board in 1994. In 1995, he divorced his wife and married this person. But wait, there's more. In 1995, his ex-wife met someone, also on a Prodigy Bulletin Board and ... married him last month! What is going on here?!?

In thinking about such accounts, I began to wonder how often they occurred and whether or not they compared favorably to relationships established in more traditional settings. To find out, I e-mailed a survey to a random sample of one thousand students who had Internet accounts at a local university. Of the 248 who returned the survey, eighty-eight (36%) indicated they had formed a friendship with another individual in an online setting. Nineteen (22%) described it as a close romantic relationship.[25]

The sizeable number of online relationships that were apparently formed by this group of students surprised me. Based on current theory, it seems unlikely that two individuals would ever form a close relationship on the Internet. Most such accounts highlight the importance of physical proximity and frequent face-to-face interaction. They also underscore the importance of social cues, especially the role of physical attraction. In spite of the absence of both, an unexpectedly large number of close friendships were formed on the Internet. Of course, most theories of close relationships were formulated well before the development of electronic communication. It is clearly time to undertake a thoroughgoing overhaul of them now.

I also wondered whether or not the students' online relationships differed from those formed in more traditional settings. To answer this question, I e-mailed a second survey to the individuals who said they had formed a close romantic relationship on the Internet. The twelve students who returned this survey reported their relationships moved quite readily from cyberspace to real space. All of them had exchanged phone numbers, half were either dating casually or exclusively, and two of the twelve said they were either engaged or planning to be married. There was also an overwhelming consensus among them that their online romances were just as strong, if not stronger, and just as satisfying as those they had formed offline. Far from being shallow, it was clear that they had formed genuinely close relationships of considerable depth on the Internet.

The students also confirmed much of what Daum described in her *New Yorker* tale. Most said it much easier to talk online than in face-to-face conversations. The online world was a safe place where they felt comfortable disclosing personal details of their life and where they found a ready audience for their personal narratives. They did not find the technology dehumanizing. In fact, many claimed it gave rise to *more authentic* experiences than most of their ordinary, day-to-day encounters.

I was not surprised to hear this, as it is sometimes difficult for me to make casual conversation in the real world. But in cyberspace, the words seem to flow; I am not the least bit hesitant to speak frankly or in a carefree fashion. No one is going to conk me on the head or frown at me for doing so. Occasionally my correspondent doesn't even know who I am. It is a place where I am relaxed and strangely more spontaneous than I tend to be in public.

The controlled pace of e-mail conversation also appeals to me. In composing an e-mail, I can organize my thoughts methodically and edit them as I go along. Sometimes I will simply start a message then save it in draft form until I am ready to finish or expand it before sending it on its way. I am alone in my study and it is quiet, my books are nearby and I can mull over what I want to say with far greater ease than I can in a public situation.

When viewed this way, the online setting is simply another place to meet people and maintain contact with friends. It is also a place where the conversation can be deeper and more coherent then it is in face-to-face encounters. Instead of going to a bar or party to meet someone, you can do so now by sitting comfortably at your desk without worrying about making a fashion statement or enduring yet another traffic jam.

Because your exchange can be saved and printed, it is also less fleeting than it is in ordinary conversation. I have found this kind of dialogue to be great fun, unexpectedly provocative at times, and have taken to it with an apparent natural gusto. Jeff Bezos, the founder of Amazon.com, once remarked: "I love e-mail. I think it is changing the world." I don't know about the world at large. But I do know it has certainly changed my world. And when my server goes down as it has been doing quite often lately, or when there is no one for me to send an e-mail, I become more than a little bit unglued.

Notes

22   Wendy Less·r. 1999. *The Amateur: An Independent Life of Letters*. Random House: New York

23   Vivian Gornick. 1996. *Approaching Eye Level*. Beacon Press: Boston.

24   Megham Daum, August 25, 1977. *The New Yorker*.

25   Analysis of the data indicated that perhaps as many as 76 in every 1,000 students who had Internet accounts may have formed a close online romance.

RESEARCH

There may be some kinds of knowledge that science and technology will never deliver. When we ask science to move beyond explaining how things (say, hurricanes) generally behave to predicting exactly how a particular thing (say, Thursday's storm off the South Carolina coast) will behave, we may be asking it to do more than it can. No hurricane is quite like any other hurricane. Although all hurricanes follow predictable laws of behavior, each one is continuously shaped by myriad uncontrollable, accidental factors in the environment.

Atul Gawande

THE
ENLIGHTENMENT
EFFECT

*I don't mean to say that thinking and reaching
decisions have no influence on behavior. But
behavior does not merely enact whatever has
already been thought through and decided. It
has its own sources, and is my behavior, quite
independently, just as my thoughts are my
thoughts, and my decisions my decisions.*

Bernard Schlink

In 1964, Kitty Genovese was brutally attacked and killed
in New York City in the presence of 38 individuals who
observed her killer stalk and stab her in three separate
attacks over the course of a half hour. Not one of the 38
bystanders came to her aid or called the police before
she was killed. This incident "shook" the soul of New
York and galvanized social psychologists into a
program of research on the failure of bystanders to come
to the aid of distressed individuals.

I always spend a good deal of time reviewing this
research in my social psychology class. Last year, after

we had completed our discussion, a student wrote to me about an experience she had while driving to the university one day. She said she had always considered herself a helpful person and that when we had discussed the Kitty Genovese case in class, she found it hard to believe that no one had come to her aid or even called the police. She told me that she was the daughter of a retired police officer and had learned from a very early age to help others when she could and, in fact, had often come to the aid of individuals in distress. She added that she liked to believe that she'd help in almost any situation. She then recounted the following experience:

> "I dropped off my daughter at her childcare and hurried off to school. I had a mid-term to take at 8 A.M. and I had to get to the park-and-ride pronto, before I missed my morning bus. I was *running late* [Italics mine] and knew that bus was the only way I'd get to school on time. As I crossed an intersection, I noticed an accident off to my left... My instincts said, 'Go see if anyone is hurt!' but I was in a hurry to get to my mid-term. I found myself driving down the road on the way to take a silly test, instead of stopping to help people who could have been seriously injured."

The student recalled how she had invoked all sorts of justifications for her inaction as she was driving by the accident. She reported there were other people on the road who she thought would stop to help or use their cell phone to call for assistance. The accident didn't appear to be that serious, so she thought the people were probably fine and would only be irritated by her interference. Finally, she said her mid-term exam was important and she wasn't sure if the instructor would allow her to make up for it.

Although she made it to the exam on time, she was troubled by the experience. In thinking back over it, she felt that none of the excuses justified her failure to intervene. She recalled the many studies we had considered in class about the failure of bystanders to come to the aid of distressed individuals. In one, seminary students, on their way to deliver a speech on the Good Samaritan, passed right by a victim slumped in a doorway when they had to hurry to arrive on time for their talk.[26] She recognized that this study had much in common with her own experience. In both instances, the need to hurry somewhere had taken precedence over behaving helpfully. She concluded her note with this comment:

> "I had an added factor that is important to mention. I knew of the studies and had that information in my mind, even as I drove past the accident. I took the time to mentally note that my situation resembled the seminary student study. *Prior knowledge* [Italics mine] of helping behaviors or non-helping behaviors didn't cause me to stop and help. At most, that knowledge simply caused me to recognize my behavior and reflect on it."

I was taken aback by the intelligence of her remark. For it confronts squarely one of the most vexing questions in the behavioral and social sciences: Does scientific knowledge influence future behavior? The student hoped that it would, hoped that she would be more likely to help in the future in light of what she had learned about the bystander problem. At the same time, she admitted that she wasn't sure she would and that even *knowing* about the research on the bystander problem would not overcome the influence of more pressing demands.

The student's prediction about her own behavior flies in the face of ordinary beliefs about the role of knowledge and information on behavior. Ask anyone in advertising or marketing, for example. Almost without exception, the communication campaigns designed by the individuals in these fields are information intensive, in spite of all the evidence demonstrating that, by itself, information often has very little or no impact on behavior.

The "enlightenment effect" is the term Kenneth Gergen, a social psychologist, has given to the effect of scientific knowledge on behavior. According to Gergen, knowledge about social psychological research "liberates" one from its influence. With respect to helping behavior, Gergen puts it this way, " ... knowing that persons in trouble are less likely to be helped when there are large numbers of bystanders may increase one's desire to offer his services under such conditions."[27]

Gergen suggests this can happen for any one of three reasons. He claims, for example, that psychological principles tend to be prescriptive, that is, they tell us how we should behave. In the future, armed with this information, we might want to behave in the ways the principles indicate are desirable, say, by helping another person in distress. Secondly, knowledge of psychological findings can sensitize us to alternative courses of action, so we will not be so constrained in responding, when we are subsequently placed in a comparable situation. Finally, Gergen suggests that sometimes individuals come to *resent* the control implied by psychological principles. After learning about them, they may attempt to reassert their freedom by acting contrary to their behavioral implications.

Do we behave any differently once we know about psychological research than we would if we had not been so informed? Fortunately, the question lends itself to empirical research. A few years ago, with the help of a college senior working on her senior thesis, I decided to conduct a field experiment on knowledge of the bystander problem. I wanted to find out if students at a local high school would be more likely to help a person in need if they had studied the bystander problem than if they hadn't. I also wanted to find out if their willingness to help would vary as a function of how much they knew about the research. To do so, I selected four classes and varied the amount of information the students in each were given about the bystander problem.

One group, the high information condition, was shown two films that explored the research on helping behavior. They also read a journal article on the bystander problem, discussed both the films and the article in class, and were asked to write a brief essay on the topic. Another group, the moderate information condition, viewed only one of the films and discussed it briefly afterwards. The third group, low information condition, simply saw the film without discussion. Finally, these three groups were compared with a control group of students who were not given any information about the bystander problem.

The day after the films were shown, the students were asked to take a brief psychological test in another part of the school. As they were on their way to the testing room, they were confronted with an individual who needed assistance. Half of the students passed by a confederate who dropped a load of books in the hallway, while the other half passed a wheezing confederate who was staging an asthma attack on a stairway.

The outcome of the study was clear.[28] Only about 50% of the students stopped to help the confederate, regardless of whether it took the form of picking up dropped books or asking the asthma victim if there was anything they could do to help. More importantly, the amount of information individuals had about the bystander problem had no influence on the likelihood that they would render assistance. Students in the high information condition were no more likely to help than students in the control or other treatment conditions. In this experiment then, having been informed that bystanders often fail to come to the aid of distressed individuals and, in some cases reading and discussing the topic with their classmates, did not lead these students to be any more helpful than those who had not been so informed.

This is not an isolated finding. It has been observed in a surprising number of other situations where individuals who have been informed of psychological research do not behave any differently than those who are naive with respect to this information. In a striking study, Shelton gave subjects complete information about Stanley Milgram's well-known experiments[29] on obedience and disobedience in which subjects appear to inflict increasingly severe pain on others when they were asked to by an authority. After giving her subjects a detailed account of Milgram's methods and research findings, Shelton asked them to serve as experimenters in a similar study. Of her 24 informed subjects, only 1 resisted the demands of the authority to continue the experiment in spite of the clearly visible distress of the confederates in her study. She says:

> "For these participants, knowing that people are willing to coerce others and cause distress to obtain a scientific understanding and feeling the original Milgram study to be personally distasteful, did not preclude behaving in a manner similar to that obtained in the original Milgram study."

The increasing public awareness of Milgram's research provides an additional test of the enlightenment effect. His research has been widely written about in the media, portrayed in television plays and films, and was the subject of at least one popular song. The studies have been discussed in countless public forums and many academic disciplines. Milgram's work is as well-known as any program of research in psychology. If, as a result of this dissemination process, individuals have become more "enlightened" about unreasonable demands of authority, one might expect a diminution in the overall level of obedience in ensuing replications of his work. However, a recent analysis of these replications, which covered a 20-year period, from 1963 to 1983, found no systematic decline in obedience during this time. The overall level of obedience in the most recent studies was just as high (65% of the subjects) as it was in the earlier ones. [30]

The enlightenment effect has been explored in many other situations. Investigators have given individuals a good deal of information about the "risky shift" that occurs in group decision-making situations. This effect refers to the fact that a group of individuals often makes riskier decisions than individuals who are asked to decide the issue alone. Giving individuals in a group setting complete information about the risky shift did not make their decision any less risky than it was when they had no knowledge of the effect.[31]

In another study, investigators examined the role of knowing about the primacy effect in forming an impression of another individual. This effect refers to the fact that personal adjectives appearing at the beginning of a list used to form an impression of someone else have more influence than adjectives at the end of the list. Informing individuals about the primacy effect had no influence on the ratings they formed of an individual in a subsequent impression-forming task.[32]

These findings are consistent with recent research on informing individuals about common errors and biases in making social judgments. For example, in a recent study individuals were told about research findings on the hindsight bias—the tendency of individuals to overestimate the accuracy of their prior judgments. The participants in these experiments were given information about the hindsight bias and full details of the experimental procedures that they would experience. The task required them to answer difficult questions that called for numerical estimates. After completing this task, they were given the answers to the questions and then asked to recall their initial estimates. The amount of bias they displayed in recalling their *initial* judgments was unaffected by their knowledge of the hindsight bias, nor were they less biased than the participants who had no knowledge of the bias.[33] In both cases, individuals tended to overestimate the accuracy of their earlier estimates.

The increasing application of compliance techniques in sales and marketing situations led me to conduct one other test of the enlightenment effect. As compliance techniques have become more sophisticated and increasingly subject to misuse, I have been led to wonder if there is anything a person can do to resist their influence. Robert Cialdini, who has carried out an influential program of research on compliance techniques, has argued that greater awareness of the principles of compliance is our strongest defense. He suggests that recognizing when such techniques are being used and knowing something about how they work should help individuals to resist their influence.[34]

To test Cialdini's notion, I asked individuals to participate in an experiment in which they were first asked to prepare for a reading comprehension test by reading materials on compliance techniques. One group read sections of one of Cialdini's studies on the Low Ball technique in which a target request to comply is preceded by a *less* costly one. Another group read an experiment he had conducted on the Reciprocal Concession technique, in which the target request to comply is preceded by a *more* costly one. The control group read a report that had nothing to do with compliance techniques.

As they were nearing the end of the reading comprehension test, the participants were interrupted by a confederate who attempted to gain their compliance on another task by employing either the Low Ball or Reciprocal Concession procedure. A little over a week later, these two procedures were employed once again during a telephone call, which asked the participants to complete a survey about the recent Presidential election.

We found that individuals who knew about either compliance technique were just as likely to comply as those who had not been previously informed.[35] Thus, we could find no support for Cialdini's claim that knowing about compliance principles will protect individuals from their influence. At least this knowledge was not sufficient to defend against the compliance pressures employed in this situation.

Taken together then, it appears that the doubts expressed by the student in my social psychology class about the influence of scientific knowledge were well founded. She had hoped that information she acquired about the bystander problem would make her a more helpful person and that something as trivial as a test or social obligation would not take precedence over the health and welfare of others. However, she wasn't entirely sure that it would and she knew that she would probably be largely influenced by conditions in the immediate social situation—her own schedule and the presence of other people.

A lifetime of studying psychology has convinced me that this point of view is essentially correct, that all too often we overestimate the influence of thinking on behavior. As we have seen, knowledge of social psychological principles does not appear to have a strong effect on behavior. Instead, it represents only one of the many factors that influence behavior, especially in situations where there are powerful external pressures. In these situations, individuals may find it very difficult to translate their knowledge into action.

The task before us now is to learn how to overcome this effect, to learn how to make our knowledge more salient in those situations where it might prove useful. This often occurs naturally, when, for example, newly acquired information is still readily available. However, the information becomes less and less available with the passage of time. Individuals then need to be reminded with a personal appeal or a conspicuous signal, or learn how to prompt themselves in those situations where the information is clearly applicable. Once its relevance is recognized, individuals may be more likely to bring their knowledge to bear on their actions. Until we develop more effective ways to accomplish this, we must be careful not to overestimate the extent to which a psychologically informed public will behave any differently than an uninformed one.

Notes

26 Darley, J. & Batson, D. (1973). "From Jerusalem to Jericho:" A study of situational and dispositional variables in helping behavior. *Journal of Personality and Social Psychology*, 27, 100-108. In this experiment, theological students were asked to give a talk on job opportunities for seminary students, or the parable of the Good Samaritan. While walking to another building to give their talk (either late or on time), they passed a victim (coughing and groaning) slumped in an alleyway. The theological students going to give a talk on the parable of the Good Samaritan were no more likely to help than those giving a talk on job prospects for seminary students. *Thinking* about the Good Samaritan did not increase helping behavior. Being in a *hurry* decreased it.

27 Gergen, K. 1973, Social Psychology as History. *Journal of Personality and Social Psychology*, 26, 309-320.

28 Katzev, R & Averill, A. 1984. Knowledge of the bystander problem and its impact on subsequent helping behavior. *Journal of Social Psychology*, 123, 223-230.

29 Shelton, G. A. (1982). The generalization of understanding to behavior: The role of perspective in enlightenment. Unpublished doctoral dissertation, University of British Columbia, Vancouver, Canada.

30 Blass, T (2000). The Milgram paradigm after 35 years: Some things we now know about obedience to authority. In Thomas Blass (Ed) Obedience to Authority: Current Perspectives on the Milgram Paradigm. Mahwah, New Jersey: Lawrence Erlbaum Associates.

31 Bermant, G. & Starr, M. (1972). Telling people what they are likely to do: Three experiments. In *Proceedings of the 80th Annual Convention of the American Psychological Association*. Washington, DC: American Psychological Association.

32 ibid.

33 Pohl, R. F. & Hell, W. (1996) No reduction in hindsight bias after complete information and repeated testing. *Organizational Behavior and Human Decision Processes*, 67, 49-58.

34 Cialdini, R. B. (1985). *Influence: Science and Practice*. Glenview, Il: Foresman.

35 Katzev, R. & Brownstein, R. (1989). The influence of enlightenment on compliance. *Journal of Social Psychology*, 129, 335-347.

EFFECTS OF READING LITERATURE

One's life is more formed, I sometimes think,
by books than by human beings . . .

Graham Greene

I'll never forget the first novel I read from start to finish in a day. I can't be sure how old I was, perhaps 14 or 15, about the time I was in high school. The book was Alexander Dumas' *Camille*. As I recall the situation, the 1937 movie with Greta Garbo as Camille had been reissued and for reasons that completely baffle me now, I decided that I wanted to see it. I am fairly certain my mother suggested I should read the book first and that she had purchased a copy for me.

And so, after breakfast early one weekend morning, I went back to bed to begin reading the novel. Going back to bed after breakfast was not something I ever did. That day was *the* exception and other than when I have been ill, I've never done it again. Reading *Camille* during the day in bed seemed like such a lark, thoroughly in tune with the spirit of the story. Everything seemed to fall into place then on what was no doubt a sunny Saturday in Los Angeles sometime during the early fifties.

I returned to bed after lunch and continued reading until I had finished by mid-afternoon, in plenty of time to see the film that evening. It was showing at a nearby art house and I know that I went alone. Now, some fifty years later, tales of ill-fated romances and their screen adaptations continue to exert a powerful hold on me. Indeed, the widespread popularity of this literary genre in general indicates that I am far from alone in this regard.

Yet we hear from every quarter that no one reads anymore, that television and now the Web have all but killed off the pleasures of the page. We bemoan the closing of one bookstore after another. However, I am growing increasingly dubious of all these obituaries for reading. In truth, informal book clubs and reading groups are flourishing throughout the country.

As a case in point, consider my hometown. Portland, Oregon is said to be rather bookish, with perhaps more bookstores per capita than any other comparably sized city in the country. People seem to like to read. Or at least to have books around for those long and endless rainy days and nights. In a recent edition of the *Sunday Oregonian,* there was a list of Book Groups scheduled to meet during the month. Sometimes they met weekly but more often than not once a month.

I counted twenty-four different groups and those were just the ones whose meetings were open to the public. I was astonished. The Great Books Group. The Popular Fiction Book Group. The Modern Women's Group, Contemporary Fiction, Science Fiction, and Gay, Lesbian, and Bisexual Book Groups. The Romance

Readers Classic Books, First Wednesday, Mystery Lovers, Memoir, and Biography Groups. On and on the list went. I was simply bowled over by the number of groups, the range of topics, and the fact that they were meeting regularly. Who would have imagined that so many people were doing so much reading?

Late in August 2001, Chicago launched a reading program in which every adult and adolescent in the city was asked to read the same book. Harper Lee's *To Kill a Mockingbird* was the book that was chosen and from all accounts, the program was an enormous success, as organized discussions were carried out by private clubs, employee groups, reading clubs, as well as informal gatherings at Starbucks. The idea for a community-wide reading project apparently started in Seattle and has since spread to other cities, including San Francisco, Los Angeles, and most recently New York, a city with millions of readers, where a committee is currently engaged in a vigorous debate about which book to select.

Recently I have begun to wonder how readers are influenced by programs like this and by their reading experiences, in general. How has their life or personality been affected by the reading they have been doing? To find out, I began by looking for empirical studies that have examined the effects of reading literature, as well as the writing of critics who, I was sure, have given a good deal of thought to the matter. I was amazed at what I discovered. In a word, I could not find any systematic research on this topic. Thinking I had not been searching in the right places, I sent the following e-mail to a listserv in psychology dedicated to literature and the arts:

Dear Group Members:

I have joined the Div 10 Listserv because of my interest in literature and psychology. Specifically, I am interested in how reading literature, both fiction and non-fiction, influences behavior and personality. I have had little success in locating previous empirical research or analysis . . . of this question. Thus, I seek your help in obtaining information about studies that have investigated this issue. Once collected I will post a summary of citations to the Listserv.

Richard Katzev, Ph.D.

I received only one reply that read in part as follows:

Dear Dr. Katzev:

In my 1977 Book, "Psychology and Literature" (Chicago: Nelson-Hall), I reviewed some of the literature on the influence of literature reading on development and cognition, but I'm afraid the material is discursive/anecdotal rather than empirical. The problem is designing a controlled study, holding as much as possible constant, to see what effect literature had. However, the discursive literature is pretty interesting, all things considered.

Martin Lindauer

Moreover, it appears the question has also been virtually ignored by literary critics who, to my astonishment, seem to have examined almost everything else about literature except its influence on readers. Robert Wilson[36] put it well: "Although most persons would agree that reading may be generally efficacious in directing an individual's development, few attempts have been made to define its influence more precisely."

Perhaps the question is simply too complex or too psychological for the critics. They may simply assume that reading literature influences individuals, that, indeed, it has enormous impact on their thought and personality, and that it is hopelessly naive to even question this belief, let alone to inquire about the nature and extent of literature's influence.

To be sure, many authors have given *personal* accounts of books that have shaped their lives and writing. In *How to Read and Why*, Harold Bloom[37] claims that ultimately " ... we read to strengthen the self, and to learn its authentic interests". Anna Quindlen sounds a similar note in *How Reading Changed My Life*.[38] "All of reading is really only finding ways to name ourselves, and, perhaps, to name the others around us so that they will no longer seem like strangers."

We sometimes hear of books that have exerted a major influence on someone's life or the lives of a large group of individuals. Goethe's *Sorrows of Young Werther* is perhaps the foremost example of the powerful impact of the reading experience. *Werther* led so many young individuals into acts of imitative suicide that it was banned in several countries soon after it was published.

Occasionally the *Oregonian* runs a column, "One Book That Changed Your Life," in the Sunday book section, where individuals describe the way in which they have been influenced by a notable book or reading experience. One person described how the zest for life of Lee Mellon, the hero of Richard Brautigan's *A Confederate General From Big Sur,* led him into a career of bookseller. Another wrote of a book that finally helped him overcome a lifetime of alcohol addiction.

The San Francisco bookstore, A Clean Well-Lighted Place for Books, has a page on its website (*www.bookstore.com/bookschallenge.htm*) that invites readers to "name the book that changed your life." One contributor responded: "The Harry Potter books changed my life. I used to hate reading. Now I am the best reader in the class. Those books changed my imagination. I wasn't too much of a dreamer. Now, I love to imagine things. I just hope that they change someone else's life like they did mine."

The Autodidactic Press also has a similar invited "Books that Changed Lives" page on its website (*www.autodidactic.com/changedlives.htm*). In citing *The Autobiography of Malcolm X,* one individual wrote: "I first read the book as a sixth grader. The book was so searing that I vowed to become like that unusual man. Today I am a Muslim as a direct result of Malcolm's autobiography."

However, rather than personal testimonials of this sort, I was looking for more general tests of the hypotheses that Bloom and Quindlen had proposed, tests that measured the varied effects of literary experiences on readers. Do other individuals derive their sense of personal identity from the literature they read and, if so, how widespread is this effect? How durable is such an effect and how does it compare to the many other ways we learn about ourselves?

My search uncovered several investigations of the use of literature as a therapeutic tool. This approach, known as "bibliotherapy," is the "use of print and nonprint material, whether imaginative or informational . . . to effect changes in emotionally disturbed behavior."[39] While bibliotherapy was employed initially with individuals who were institutionalized in prison or mental hospitals, it has recently been extended to other community settings including schools and libraries. All such programs try to use the experience of reading literature to change a person's behavior, attitudes or values in some way.

Is bibliotherapy an effective way to change behavior? The behaviorally-oriented approaches, where individuals are asked to read self-help materials in treating problems such as alcoholism, obesity, and social anxiety, appears to be the most successful. In contrast, reading fiction, poetry or creative non-fiction appears to have only a modest degree of influence that is most clearly reflected in attitude rather than behavioral change. However, the research in this area is not extensive and what has been done is methodologically far from elegant.

The most direct attempt to answer the question I was grappling with is a program ambitiously known as Changing Lives Through Literature. It is designed as a sentencing alternative for high-risk offenders who have a large number of prior convictions.[40] In addition, the program is restricted to offenders who express a willingness to participate in lieu of a jail sentence.

Changing Lives Through Literature is based on the belief that criminal offenders can derive considerable benefit from the experience of reading and discussing major works of literature. Robert Waxler, one of its founders, suggests that " . . . offenders often commit criminal acts because they operate from a value system that gives priority to emotions and primal instinct, rather than to reason and critical thinking. We need to challenge that single-minded value system by using novels and short stories that unfold the complexity and diversity of character and human consciousness."[41]

The program tries to achieve this goal with intensive reading and group discussions of contemporary literature, including works such as Bank's *The Affliction*, Dickey's *Deliverance*, Ellison's *Invisible Man*, Hemingway's *The Old Man and the Sea*, London's *Sea Wolf*, Mailer's *An American Dream* and Morrison's *The Bluest Eye*. The discussion sessions take place every other week for two hours.

In a study of the first four groups of offenders, the recidivism rate of 32 men who completed the course was compared with a matched group of 40 probationers who were not exposed to any aspect of the program.[42] An analysis of follow-up criminal records indicated that only 6 of the 32 men in the reading group (18.8%) were convicted on new charges after completing the program. In the comparison group, 18 of the 40 men (45%), three times more than the reading group, were convicted on new charges during this period.

While these differences are important, it is not entirely clear they can be attributed to the *specific* works that were read or to the reading experience itself, independent of its content. The differences could also be due to the group discussions or the contact the offenders had with each other, as well as the group leader.[43] Moreover, the attempt to match the groups was not successful, as those in the reading group had more prior convictions and were rated as more motivated to "make changes in their lives" than members of the comparison group. Without further tests, that ideally should include a control group of offenders who read non-literary materials, these factors cannot be ruled out as possible explanations for the initial findings.

In spite of this uncertainty, the Changing Lives Through Literature program impressed me. It sought to measure objectively the effects of literary experiences. It did so in a formidable setting with a group of individuals who are not often responsive to recidivism reduction techniques. Perhaps the offenders did gain some insight about their own behavior from the readings and discussions after all. As one of the participants reported: "I started to see myself in him [the ship captain in Sea Wolf] and I didn't like what I saw."

Unfortunately this was the only empirical study that I could find on the effects of reading literature *per se*. It appears that academic interest in this question is restricted to anecdotal reports of individual scholars or the analysis of the literary influences on particular writers. Charles Darwin described a paradigm case of this kind in recalling how Thomas Malthus' *An Essay on the Principle of Population* influenced his own work.

> I happened to read for amusement Malthus
> on *Population,* and being well prepared to
> appreciate the struggle for existence which
> everywhere goes on from long-continued
> observations of the habits of animals and
> plants, it at once struck me that under these
> circumstances favourable variations would
> tend to be preserved and unfavourable ones
> to be destroyed. The result of this would be
> the formation of a new species. Here, then, I
> had at last got a theory by which to
> work .... [44]

In commenting on this example, Edwin Castagna noted:

> This was one of the most significant reading
> experiences in the history of science. A bright
> light had been kindled in the brain of an
> obscure young scientist. The tinder was a
> book in another field. Where can one find a
> clearer or more convincing illustration of the
> powerful impact of reading on intellectual
> progress?[45]

It appears that the effort to determine the effects of
reading on the life and work of individuals will have
to be content with examples of this sort. Some have
claimed that even trying to answer this question in a
more systematic manner is folly, that it is impossible to
disentangle the various effects of reading experiences.
Others have suggested it is unlikely that literature of
any form can change a person's life, but that every now
and then, a book comes along that simply reinforces
the way the person already thinks and acts.

The truth probably lies somewhere in between these extremes. Lorrie Moore put it this way: "Everything one reads is nourishment of some sort—good food or junk food—and one assumes it all goes in and has its way with your brain cells." When put this way, I think most persons could hardly take issue with such a claim, that even though it is difficult to say much more, they are surely influenced in one way or another by the literature they read, no doubt by some books more than others. Unfortunately, the apparent complexity of this process has discouraged researchers from investigating it more deeply. Yet, it is clearly one of sufficient importance to call forth an active program of empirical study, one where an effort will be made to identify the effects of the literary experience in terms that are a good deal more specific than "way with your brain cells."

Notes

36 Robert N. Wilson, Literary Experience and Personality. *Journal of Aesthetics and Art Criticism*, 1956, 14, 47-57.

37 Harold Bloom. *How to Read and Why*. New York: Scribner, 2000.

38 Anna Quindlen. *How Reading Changed My Life*. New York: Ballantine Published Group, 1998.

39 Richard J. Riordan & Linda S. Wilson. Bibliotherapy: Does It Work? *Journal of Counseling and Development*, 1989, 67, 506-508.

40 The average number of prior convictions for the first two groups of male participants was 18.4 per person.

41 Robert Waxler. Why Literature?: The Power of Stories. Online document: *http:// www.ed.gov/offices/ OVAE/OCE/ SuccessStories/Part2.htm*.

42 G. Roger Jarjoura & Susan T. Krumholz. Combining Bibliotherapy and Positive Role Modeling as an Alternative to Incarceration. *Journal of Offender Rehabilitation*, 1998, 28, 127-139.

43 The groups were led by a rotating group of individuals, including a college professor, probation officer, and a judge.

44 Cited in Edwin Castagna. *Caught in the Act: The Decisive Reading of Some Notable Men and Women and Its Influence on Their Actions and Attitudes.* Metuchen, New Jersey: The Scarecrow Press, 1982

45 ibid.

THE CAR SHARING REVOLUTION

This car sharing thing . . . it looks like it just might work.

Susan Hauser

Dear Environment:

I sold my car the other day. I had been wanting to for quite some time. It wasn't easy. My car was quite a machine. Too fancy, some said. I loved to drive it. But it was time to change. Time to act. Time to do something about the way the car has ruined our cities and much of the nearby countryside. It was time to turn away from all that and see if it was possible to get along without a car. In reply to your query, I am sending you this log of how it has been going.

June 18: I expected to be in a funk. I wasn't. In truth, I felt a certain liberation. Need to check the taxi company phone numbers. Ditto for the car rental agencies. Check the bus routes and time schedules. Wonder where the bus stops downtown, how long it takes, what I might do en route?

June 20: It has been warm, making everything much easier. Walk for coffee. Walk to market. Walk to post office. Delightful. Must think about planning more carefully. Make a list of things do to. Do them all at once with A's car, rather than one at a time. Planning is everything. Lists are everything.

June 21: It rained, so I used A's car for an errand. I could have walked. But didn't. I will have to try harder.

June 23: There was little need for the car again. I am reminded that most of the time it simply sat in the garage. Suspect it was used on the average about a half-hour or less each day. Some days not at all. Those are primarily in the summer. No doubt the real test will come in the winter.

July 2: The days drift by without difficulty. Every now and then, I take A's car for an errand. To the market, a meeting, and once to buy an airline ticket. The car is convenient but not necessary. One day I actually took the bus downtown to Fed Ex a letter. Just for the experience. The wait for the bus seemed long, although it could not have been more than 10-12 minutes. The walk to the Fed Ex office was entertaining, with a bookstore on the way. The return trip was easy with only a momentary wait for the bus this time. The entire expedition from start to finish took no more than an hour and a half. No sweat, on a tolerably pleasant summer afternoon, with no pressing deadlines.

July 10: All is going well. The weather remains pleasant. I walk everywhere or wait until A's car is free. I try to arrange meetings at home. So far so good. Tomorrow I rendezvous with A for a weekend in the Cascades. I will take the bus to our meeting place out of town. I'll probably taxi to the bus station first, although I could walk if I leave early. Perhaps there's a bus to the bus station.

July 29: I have been car-less for days now and have not felt the need for one. I would like to get to the bank, but have been using the cash machine instead. The other night I actually took the bus to see a film. I studied the bus schedule and went to the bus stop at the appointed time. It arrived soon thereafter. Transferred to another and was dropped off a short distance from the theater. It wasn't so difficult. To be sure it took a bit longer. And I took a taxi back. But I did it! It was my premier going-to-a-film-on-the-bus performance.

August 21: It is August now and I have been traveling. Who needs a car then?

September 17: It is getting colder now. A is away a good deal of the time. I am not looking forward to being car-less as the winter approaches. At times I would just like to go to a film, visit the library or a distant bookstore. Anywhere. I know I could take the bus or rent a car. Next time.

September 26: My tale must come to an end. I have succumbed to the weather, to the temptations of modern life, and to the perpetual absence of A and her car. I am sorry, dear Environment, you will have to find a better man than I. But it became too much of a hassle to go anywhere. More often than not, I simply didn't. Lectures were missed. Films came and went. Errands were continually postponed. I love being a recluse, but not exclusively. Every now and then I need and want to sally forth quickly and conveniently. So I bought a sporty runabout today. Not my usual chariot. But every bit as spiffy with all the whistles and bells.

Could I have done anything different? I did try the alternatives—bus, taxi, walking, and waiting patiently. Maybe if I was younger and more carefree, I could manage the delay and inconvenience they entail. But the additional travel time and blasts of cold rain during the long days of winter finally did me in. I suppose I should have waited for the new car sharing organization that will be starting up soon. Maybe I could manage that. Must remember to check it out.

Yours for less traffic,
Richard Katzev

This year, *Money Magazine* ranked Portland as number one in its list of the Best Places to live in the United States. It is not the first time Portland has been so "honored." Much of the praise that has descended on Portland lately comes from the long tradition of land-use planning that exists in the region. However, in spite of all that has been done to control the area's growth, the automobile has taken over our landscape, much as it has everywhere else in this country. Our countryside is cluttered with highways and urban sprawl. Cars, roadways, and garages dominate the downtown sections of the city. Portland has serious air pollution alerts during the summer. And during commute times there is as much congestion here as in any major metropolitan area.

During the past decade, those of us who live and work here have been inundated with information urging us to take the bus, walk, ride a bike, or carpool, instead of driving our car to work alone. In spite of all this publicity, far more of us commute to work alone today than in the 1980s. The overall level of carpooling and transit ridership has decreased during this period, as well. These trends are discouraging. Unfortunately, much the same has occurred in most large cities in this country. It is abundantly clear that we are making very little headway in solving the many problems that the automobile, in spite of all of its delights, has brought to our communities.

These problems cannot be taken lightly. Automobile usage is responsible for up to 60% of the air pollution in the United States, as well as pervasive noise pollution in most urban communities. Automobiles are a major source of carbon dioxide, the so-called greenhouse gas that is thought to be the major contributor to global warming. The automobile has drastically reshaped our urban environment, with between 25% and 30% of urban land devoted to roads, parking spaces, and other automobile facilities. The automobile uses enormous amounts of natural resources, including the materials (steel, rubber, zinc) used in its construction, the petroleum required to fuel it, and the materials used to build and maintain the highway and roadway system in this country.

Then there are the very steep costs involved in owning and operating a car. The latest American Automobile Association analysis indicates it can cost anywhere from $4,400 to $8,500 (including fuel, insurance, financing, license, and depreciation) per year to own a relatively inexpensive car. Of course, many people spend much more. Such fixed costs must be factored into the expense of any single trip, although they rarely are. Consider, for example, the cost of a ten-mile trip to the video store. Based on a 1996 estimate of 33-42 cents per mile, these fixed costs add a hidden expense of $4-$5 to the rental of the video itself. However, it is unlikely that anyone gives much thought to these costs in deciding whether or not to drive to the video store on the spur of the moment.

Finally, one cannot ignore the enormous external costs involved in maintaining the transportation system in this country. These costs are usually hidden because drivers are never directly charged for them. The costs of gasoline and vehicle registration do not cover the full costs of roadway construction and maintenance. They pay but a fraction of the costs of highway patrols, traffic management, and parking enforcement. The same is true for the heavy costs of pollution control programs or those incurred in overcoming the substantial effects it has on human health. All of these hidden costs make driving seem much cheaper than it actually is and only further encourage the needless use of automobiles.

Soon after I began conducting research on environmental problems, I realized that many, if not most of them, would continue to worsen unless individuals changed the way they used their automobiles. Yet, I had serious doubts that anything could be done to change the "deeply ingrained" driving habits of millions of Americans. In considering the various proposals put forward to accomplish this, the concept of car sharing struck me as the most promising. I recall first reading about car sharing in two newspaper articles during 1992. One described a rapidly growing car sharing organization in Berlin, while the other told of a pilot program that had operated in San Francisco for a little over a year.

Several years later, in preparing a lecture on transportation, I chanced upon the copies that I had made of those articles and immediately recognized the potential contribution that car sharing could make to the increasingly serious transportation problems facing our country. I thought car sharing would enable families with two or more cars to give up those they used infrequently. It was also clear it would make it unnecessary for individuals who did not own a car to feel they had to purchase one. I was also drawn to the concept by reports from the European car sharing groups that their members drove much less than they had before joining the organization. They were also more likely to give up their cars and use public transportation than non-members.

A car sharing organization consists of a group of individuals who share a fleet of cars much as members of a farm coop share expensive agricultural equipment or time-share owners divide the use of a resort property. Unlike auto rental fleets, the vehicles that belong to car sharing organizations are located close to where the members live, typically within three blocks of their residence.

Car sharing differs from ridesharing or carpooling in that it is not designed to transport a group of individuals to a common destination at the same time. Instead, it provides access to a vehicle at any time when walking, cycling or public transit is not possible. A variety of vehicles are usually available in the fleet to give members an efficient way to meet occasional needs, e.g. hauling, moving, transporting large groups. Car sharing also differs from conventional automobile renting in that individuals can reserve a car for short periods, charging them only for their use during that period, rather than an entire day.

To use a car, whether for an hour or a day, you simply telephone a reservation number and schedule your trip. Reservations can be made 24 hours a day, 7 days a week. Once your reservation is confirmed, you simply walk a short distance to pick up the car at one of the permanent parking sites located throughout various neighborhoods of the city. These sites are reserved solely for the vehicles owned by the car sharing organization. When a car is not available at the nearest location, another can be reserved at any of the other nearby sites.

The keys to the vehicle are usually located in a secure box at each neighborhood site that can be opened with a special key or computerized card. At the end of your trip, you simply record the distance and duration of your journey in the vehicle's log. Each month, you receive a bill based on your time and mileage usage during that period. The car sharing organization handles all maintenance, service, and repair costs, as well as insurance coverage and the cost of gasoline.

Joining a car sharing organization usually requires a fixed membership fee that is fully refundable should you decide to leave. Some organizations also have a modest non-refundable annual fee. Thereafter, you only pay when you take a trip in one of the fleet's cars. The fee scale is based on the duration of your trip and the distance traveled. For example, in Portland it is $2 per hour plus 40 cents a mile. Some organizations also offer members various package plans with rate structures based on the frequency of vehicle usage. Economically speaking, car sharing is considered to be less expensive than owning a car for individuals who drive less than 7,500 miles a year.

While car sharing has in principle operated among friends and family members since the onset of the automobile, the first formal car sharing organization was established in Switzerland in 1987. Its membership has grown steadily since then so that now it has over 50,000 members who share a fleet of almost 2,000 vehicles that are located at stations in over 350 cities and towns throughout Switzerland. The car sharing movement spread to Germany about a year later with the formation of Stadtauto ("instead of car") in Berlin and thereafter grew rapidly in Germany and other countries of Western Europe.

At the present time, there are several steadily growing car sharing organizations in North America including two well-established co-ops in British Columbia, one in Toronto and Ottawa, and a large for-profit firm in Quebec with over 2,000 members divided between Montreal and Quebec City. CarSharing Portland, launched in 1998, became the first commercial car sharing organization to be established in the United States, since a demonstration project ceased operations in San Francisco more than 10 years earlier.[46] Car sharing organizations are now operating in Seattle, San Francisco, and Boston and are on the drawing boards in several other U.S. cities including Washington, D.C. and Chicago.

The growth of car sharing in Europe and now in the United States, as well as Asia, makes it clear that the concept responds to a wide range of an individual's transportation needs. Conrad Wagner, one of the founders of the car sharing organization in Switzerland, has aptly described this rapid development.

> Ten years ago the idea of car sharing was considered just a daydream. Since then, however, car sharing has become increasingly successful and today it is one of the most significant trends in the evolution of transport and mobility.

Car sharing is clearly not for everyone. But for individuals who do not own a car or would like to cut back on one or more of their cars, car sharing offers an attractive alternative. For these people, car sharing enables them to meet their occasional, short-term transportation needs far less expensively than a taxi or rental service, and more conveniently than public transit. It also gives them access to a much greater range of vehicles, e.g. pickup, minivan, utility vehicle, than owning a single car.

In a recent evaluation of CarSharing Portland's first year of operation, I found that it appeals to a much wider range of individuals than most had anticipated. The information gathered from a survey of over one hundred of its initial members revealed that:

- Women were just as likely to become members as men.

- The average age of members was 37, with one cluster about 30 years and another at 50 years.

- Over 40% of the members were professionals in health-care or education, with approximately 20% white-collar workers in business, research or administration and fewer than 5% were students.

- The average monthly income of members was between $3,000 and $4,000 and most had graduated from college.

The early adopters of car sharing in Portland were overwhelmingly pleased with its service. Indeed, they expressed considerable pride in their membership and spoke glowingly about the organization in the following ways:

"Car sharing is incredibly convenient and very inexpensive. It definitely fits my lifestyle."

"Getting rid of my car was a lot like giving up cigarettes and I feel about as good about myself because of it. It's about as hard, but once you get free of it, a whole new world opens up of health and well-being. I have all the convenience and more, of owning a car by having ready access to [car sharing], without having to maintain it, take it to the shop, you know, deal with it."

"Having a Car Sharing Portland car within a 5 or 10-minute walk of my apartment is practically as good as having my own car on hand ... If I had kept my car, I surely would have done more driving, even when it was unnecessary."

"I like the idea of having a community car. I'm promoting being a one-car family."

The evaluation also revealed that the organization had a large influence on the member's travel behavior. Almost twenty sold a personal vehicle after joining and another third avoided purchasing one. Members also reported they became more aware of their transportation costs and began changing their customary habits by planning vehicle usage more carefully and "bundling" together trips that might have previously been taken separately or on the spur-of-the-moment. After joining CarSharing Portland, the members also reported they took the bus and rode their bicycle more often and did more walking than they had before.

Despite the overwhelming popularity of single-occupancy vehicle travel, there has never been greater need to establish car sharing organizations in the major metropolitan areas of this country. Public transportation systems continue to improve and would benefit even further by collaborating with car sharing organizations. In addition, the costs of driving, maintaining, and insuring private automobiles are steadily rising. Increasing traffic congestion and air pollution have also led many individuals to search for alternative approaches to mobility. By reducing both the number of cars and a person's dependency on them, I continue to believe that car sharing is one of the most promising.

> Dear Environment:
>
> Lo and behold, I sold my sporty runabout the other day. I truly did. I hardly ever drove it. It was absurd to keep. And so once again I am car-less.
>
> But wait. I have more to report. I finally got around to looking into the new car sharing organization here in town. It is pretty nifty. How could I not sign up? So now I have a fleet of 30 news cars at my disposal, including a pickup truck, a mini van, and, you will be pleased to learn, two hybrid vehicles that just happened to be parked a couple of blocks from my home.

I am going to give "this car sharing thing" a
try. I have a feeling I am going to be able to
pull it off this time.

Yours for the car sharing revolution,
Richard Katzev

Notes

46 Short-Term Auto Rental (STAR) was an ambitious car sharing
pilot project, which was formed in San Francisco in 1985. At
one point there were over 240 participating households and 53
cars in STAR, which were centrally located in an underground
garage within a cluster of high-rise apartment houses.
Unfortunately, as a result of unprofitable operations and poor
management, STAR folded after 18 months of what had been
planned as a 3-year project.

RECOLLECTIONS

Life, after all, is an unremitting sequence of anecdotal evidence. As individuals, that is all we have. If we are to make something of it, we must assemble, usually with the help of others, a vast array of anecdotes that can then be tested against one another and ordered according to some rational, even skeptical, scheme . . .

Samuel McCracken

IN THE COMPANY
OF SOLITUDE

*Embrace your solitude and love it ... It is through
this aloneness that you will find all your paths.*

Rilke

Not long after I had finished reading Robert Hellenga's
The Fall of the Sparrow, it dawned on me that it had much
in common with two other novels that I had read
recently, *The Archivist* by Martha Cooley, and *Black Dogs*
by Ian McEwan. Each novel depicts married couples
who appear to be generally content with one another.
Then, quite unexpectedly, they separate, with the
woman leaving in each case—two because of a
shattering emotional encounter and one because of her
increasing bouts of uncontrollable violence. Each
woman moves to a place where she lives in virtual
solitude—a convent, a home in the South of France, a
residential mental health treatment center.

Consequently, each of the men is also forced to
confront the *experience of living alone*. I take pleasure
in tales that successfully give back a reflection of my
own life or how I might wish it to be. So I was not
altogether surprised once I recognized the common

link between these three novels and the obvious reason they appealed to me. Each one touches on an experience that I, too, have confronted during the past few years, as my wife has held a job that requires her to spend a good deal of time out of town and, from time to time, I have taught at a university far from our home.

Alas, we must face this issue once again as she has been offered a prestigious academic position in another city even farther away than the one she works in now. Once more, we will have to decide if the attractive post is worth the struggle of being alone throughout the week and sometimes during the weekends, as well. We have been through all this before and while we have "come through" each time, our separations have left their mark. Besides, we are not young any more. The research on commuter marriages claims that the longer couples have been married, the less stressful they find a separation. After more than forty years of marriage, I am not the least bit convinced by this evidence.

Our dilemma is but a single example of the rapidly increasing phenomenon of solo living that appears to be settling over this country. The statistics are revealing. In 1998, 26.2 million individuals lived alone in the United States. That represented 25.6% of U.S. households, up sharply from 13% in 1960. According to the latest Census Bureau projections, by 2010, an estimated 31 million Americans will be living alone, a 40% increase from 1980. Here in Portland, solo dwellers constitute the largest proportion of household units, with approximately 36% occupied by single individuals.

The statistics take on even greater significance when broken down by age and gender. In 1998, 48% of adult women and 21% of adult men 65 years old and older lived alone. Taken together, they comprised almost 10 million individuals. It appears that at least for elderly women, living alone is the norm. Commuter marriages are also becoming increasingly common. In 1998, 7.3 million married individuals in the United States were reported to be living away from their spouses, up from 6.7 million in 1994, and 4.5 million in 1979.

In a word, several million individuals in this country live by themselves under conditions of virtual solitude throughout much of every day and night of the year. As Vivian Gornick put it:

> Who could ever have dreamed there would be so many of us floating around, those of us between thirty-five and fifty-five who live alone . . . Inevitably, the silent apartment lies in wait.[47]

What is it like to live like this? How do individuals react to the experience of living in relative isolation so much of the time?

We know from the little research that has been done and from the accounts of individuals who have written about living alone, that at times it can be a deeply longed-for experience and, at other times, a fearfully painful one. In a novel study of the effects of living alone, individuals were asked to carry electronic pagers for one week and fill out reports on their social situation and emotional state in response to signals received at random times.[48] An analysis of over 3,400 of these reports indicated that those who were unmarried and living alone spent a majority of their waking hours in solitude. Time spent alone also constituted a significant portion of the daily life of married individuals, filling 40% of their waking time.

While younger adults reported a slightly *lower* overall sense of well-being when they were alone, this was not necessarily true for older adults. For them, being alone often appeared to bring distinct advantages and was viewed as an occasion for undivided attention to reading, hobbies or their regular daily activities. Yet even for this group, especially for those who were not married, there were times when being alone was associated with considerable emotional distress.

The expression of a good deal of ambivalence also dominates the personal accounts of writers who have described the experience of living alone. The now solitary husband in Martha Cooley's *The Archivist* says:

> But once again I'd tasted solitude as an alternative to the life I was leading, and the possibility of its permanence scared and attracted me .... I found myself finally in solitude, the point at which I seem to have been aimed all along, like an arrow that after much delay had finally found its target. Naturally there are individuals with whom I have reason and desire to interact ... I am no hermit. I like the sounds of voices, the refreshment of conversation and laughter. I am fond of stimulating exchanges with particularly fine researchers. But behind or beyond these comminglings, I have safeguarded my solitude. It is essential, intact.

In reflecting on her 50 days of solitude in her home on the coast of Maine while her companion was away on business, Doris Grumbach writes:

> At first I found I missed another voice, not so much a voice responsive to my unexpressed thoughts as an independent one speaking its own words .... There was a reward for this deprivation. The absence of other voices compelled me to listen more intently to the inner one. I became aware that the interior voice, so often before stifled or stilled entirely by what I thought others wanted to hear, or what I considered to be socially acceptable, grew gratifyingly louder, more insistent. It was not that it spoke great truths or made important observation. No. It simply reminded me that it was present, saying what I had not heard it say in quite this way before .... What we yearned for were periods of solitude to renew our worn spirits.[49]

Like a teeter-totter, we oscillate back and forth between seeking solitude and, when that becomes unbearable, longing for companionship once again. It is difficult to find a level center, one where independence and attachment are in balance. Eventually we suffer in solitude and then, in turn, in togetherness. The never-ending swaying of the teeter-totter.

There have been times in my life when I have lived in virtual isolation. This experience did not come to me until I was a year or so beyond fifty, when my children had gone their separate ways and my wife had returned to graduate school in another town. Days went by when I spoke to no one.

Every afternoon I walked to the same coffeehouse, where, simply by making an appearance, I was given my "tall, no room, no lid, dash of ice." I did not find it necessary to speak to anyone while browsing at the magazine shop, the bookstore or collecting a few items at the grocery. I never felt compelled to answer the telephone. Eventually I came to realize how much of what we say during the day is totally superfluous.

I lived not unlike the Italian author Giuseppe Lampedusa whose life was sketched in a *New Yorker* profile of Palermo.

> [Lampedusa] walked every morning to the same café, where he sat in silence; then he browsed at his favorite booksellers, moved on to a second café, had lunch, came home at three and read until bedtime ... The external monotony of this routine covered and perhaps made possible an ardent inner life .... For forty years, Lampedusa once wrote, he had spent close to ten hours a day alone. Literature was his chief joy, his passion, and his solace.

I never seem to mind these long periods of isolation. At times, I actually prefer them, even to the point of viewing anyone else as an intruder. How awful that sounds. At first, I was annoyed with myself for feeling this way. Yet it did no good to resist the feeling. That was how I felt and it was impossible to ignore. Yet, eventually the feeling passed and loneliness resurfaced once again, mostly on the weekends and then mostly on Saturday. On Sunday, Monday was just a day away, so it wasn't quite so bad then.

I am not, nor do I wish to be a recluse. Occasionally, I even enjoy being with another person, usually, someone with whom I can speak openly from the very first moment, who, in turn, responds to what I say with enthusiasm and conviction, where the conversation just seems to take off. It happens much like this:

> . . . Ben pulls back out into traffic for the short drive ahead. Instantly there is between them, however slight, that elusive chemistry which occurs only occasionally when two people meet. Always a welcome surprise, it is a sort of quick familiarity, implied permission to conduct relations at a level, which is a bit deeper than the superficiality of introduction. Ben senses this and is beaming.[50]

I have enjoyed the company of only few such individuals, individuals with whom I am at once comfortable making public what is usually private. I have no idea what is responsible for this type of responsiveness. Nor does anyone else from all that I can tell. It just happens. But only rarely and then for some, never.

Again, the experience has been clearly captured in a work of fiction.

> Izumi was ten years younger than I was. We met at a business meeting. Something clicked between us the first time we laid eyes

on each other. Not the kind of thing that
happens all that often . . . . We went to a small
bar and had a few drinks. I can't recall
exactly what we talked about but we found
a million topics and could have talked
forever. With a laser-like clarity, I could grasp
everything she wanted to say. And things I
couldn't explain well to anyone else came
across to her with an exactness that took me
by surprise. We were both married, with no
major complaints about our married lives.
We loved our spouses and respect them. Still,
this was on the order of a minor miracle—
running across someone to whom you can
express your feelings so clearly, so
completely. Most people go their entire lives
without meeting a person like that. It would
have been a mistake to label this "love." It
was more like total empathy.[51]

Those who have written about this kind of conversation
claim that it is a mystery. It is said that it is not something
you can learn or try to achieve. It simply occurs. But
surely there is more to say about it, more that might be
revealed by closer inspection. However, the experience
has not, to my knowledge, ever been investigated. We
do not know if certain individuals are more likely than
others to have this experience, or if certain types of
personalities are more disposed than others to match
up this way, and we have no clue about the kind of
situations where it is most likely to occur. But if, as has
been said, the experience is "analogous to the way a
set of gears works,"[52] we will eventually come to
understand it. I am curious about it. No doubt others
are, as well. Rest assured that whatever we might one

day come to learn about this "minor miracle" will in no way affect the thrill that is to be had when it occurs.

The meeting of two minds in such an exchange is also exhausting. It is not long before it becomes wearisome and dissipating. Eventually we begin to yearn once again for the experience of solitude, for a time to concentrate, to flee the requirements of being sociable. One day, my wife and I drove back to the hometown of her university. We spent the entire hour-and-a-half drive talking to each other. Afterwards I realized how different that excursion had been from the times when I had driven the same route alone.

Together there was no chance to daydream, to speculate, to ponder the questions of the day. And so the same trip, over the same route, heading for the same place, was an altogether different experience with my wife than it was when I was alone. Either way, it can be pleasing or worthwhile, but it is always different.

Dining alone in a public restaurant has always been a treat for me. Unlike Europe, where it is a much more frequent occurrence, people who dine alone in the United States are often considered a bit odd. You are thought to be lonely or depressed, which, in turn, can be discomforting. Yet I enjoy dining alone as much as dining with companions. To be honest, I may enjoy it more. I can read, watch the crowd, get caught up in their mood, conjure up a hundred portraits. I am not distracted by the requirements of keeping up good conversation. I have to admit that, far from being a lonely experience, dining alone is often far more pleasing than dining socially.

Many discussions of solitude fail to distinguish the experience of being alone from that of being lonely. I have not found any necessary connection between the two. For some they may be closely associated, for others not. Recent research has shown quite clearly that people differ along a continuum ranging from those with a very high preference for solitude to those very low in this respect.

To be sure, there are times when loneliness will take possession of you, when circumstances become so overwhelming that everyday disposition scarcely matters at all. Yes, there are times when I am lonely, although that is just as likely to occur in a crowd, as when I am by myself. But when I am busy or deeply involved in something, the experience of loneliness never presents itself to me.

No doubt the fact that I am fundamentally content makes it possible for me to welcome the company of solitude as much as I do. So does knowing that my wife will eventually return. I can relish my solitude, answer to no one, give undivided attention to whatever I want, all in the knowledge that in due course, a day a week a month, no matter, she will drift in. To be sure then, I must try not to love the solitude too much. The best of both worlds is rarely to be had in isolation.

Notes

47 Vivian Gornick. On Living Alone. In *Approaching Eye Level*. 1996. Boston: Beacon Press.

48 Larson, R, Zuzanek, J & Mannell, Roger. 1985. Being alone versus being with people: Disengagement in the daily experience of older adults. *Journal of Gerontology*, 40, 375-381.

49 Doris Grumbach. *Fifty Days of Solitude*. 1994. Boston: Beacon Press.

50 John O'Brien. *Leaving Las Vegas*. 1990. New York: Grove Press.

51 Huruki Murakami. Man-Eating Cats. *The New Yorker*, December 4, 2000.

52 Vivian Gornick. ibid.

RECALLING MY FATHER

It doesn't matter who my father was; it matters who I remember he was.

Anne Sexton

My father died in the forty-ninth year of his life. It happened suddenly or so I was told. After I finally learned about it, it was hours before I could stop sobbing. To this day, it was the most shattering experience of my life. We were in New York when the information reached us. I remember the moment vividly. The hotel. The room. The time. The call. And then the never-ending weeping.

I was twenty-two and had just finished the first semester of graduate school at Harvard. I was not happy there and so my wife and I had left Cambridge to visit New York for a few days. We were not really clear about what we were going to do next or thinking much about it. After the call, we immediately began driving back across the country to California to be with my mother. I never did make it to my father's funeral. All this was more than 40 years ago.

I have always wondered if I was ever told the true story of his death. I have imagined that he might have taken his own life. He was so deeply depressed then and was once again living in a private psychiatric hospital. He had been through it all so often. I thought he might have simply had enough, enough of the wild highs and agonizing lows.

My father was born in 1909 in Hoboken, New Jersey soon after his parents immigrated to this country from Russia. A few years later, they moved to Alhambra, California, not far from downtown Los Angeles, where my grandfather began practicing pharmacy. I never learned why they moved to Alhambra or much about my father's time there. The little information I have about his life begins when he boldly set off to Stanford, then a virtually unknown university in Northern California, in spite of the objections of his parents, who wanted him to attend a college close to home.

He studied economics at Stanford. I once asked him if it had helped him to be a better businessman. He confessed it hadn't. While there, he developed a life-long love of Stanford sports. I recall the joy he took in recounting time and again one of the legendary victories of the Stanford football team. Those were the only tales I ever heard him tell, but at least there were those. When he died, a memorial scholarship for football players was established in his name at Stanford. Each year, I receive a very kind letter from the current holder.

When he was well, we usually took the train to Palo Alto at least once each year to watch the football team play. This seems so utterly foolish to me now. Throughout the time I was growing up, I was told I needed to do well in school so that I would be admitted to Stanford and, when it was time for me to go to college, it was the only one I applied to. In fact, I hardly knew that any others existed then.

I do not know when my father's first bout of depression occurred. I recall hearing that it might have been during his freshman year at Stanford. It was the first time he had been away from home. The details elude me and now there is no one left to answer my questions. He must have had similar bouts during the years before I entered high school, but I have no recollection of any. I find that puzzling, in light of the widespread view that such experiences usually leave a lifetime mark upon an individual. Instead, I mostly recall how outgoing he was, his generosity, and hardy laughter.

My father's name was Herbert, although I only heard his mother refer to him that way. It was said she named him after Herbert Spencer, the English philosopher of the Victorian era. That never made any sense to me since, to the best of my knowledge, she never learned to read English very well, nor did I ever see her reading anything in Russian, her native language. Most people simply called my father Herb or Herbie, as you would a close friend or buddy, which is the way most everyone felt about him.

My brother and I were raised in the first and only house that he and my mother bought in Los Angeles. They never found any reason to move from there, even though it was rather modest and a more upscale place was well within their means. It was in a quiet neighborhood of single-family dwellings, each one occupied by neighbors who were rarely seen or spoken to during the many years we lived there. I don't recall that my father spent much time at home, as each day, including the weekends, he would drive downtown to work.

He was a partner with his father and brother in a wholesale magazine distribution business in Los Angeles. In thinking about this business now, it does seem a rather odd thing to be doing. The Sunset News Company, as it was called, distributed magazines and paperbacks throughout the rapidly growing and geographically vast area of Los Angeles. Twice each week the magazines, paperbacks, and comic books that were published in this country were shipped to the firm's warehouse. The order for each bookstore, market, drugstore, bus station, airport, etc. in the region was filled by employees who collected the items and placed them on a moving assembly line. Then the order was tied into bundles and hoisted on to one of the firm's delivery trucks. Over the years, as the Los Angeles area grew almost exponentially, the Sunset News Company became something of a cash cow.

I recall the countless stacks of magazines and paperbacks (we called them "pocket books" then) that filled the warehouse, from one end to the other. On the weekends, my father would often take me to work with him and while he was in his office, I would lounge about those bundles of popular magazines and books. Some people spend their childhood lounging in fields of wildflowers. Mine was spent amongst bundles of the *Saturday Evening Post* and *Archie* comic books.

Of course, I was only able to experience this pleasure when my father was well. During much of my childhood, he was not. Yet I do not recall that his bouts of mania and depression affected me adversely, even when as a high school student, I began to appreciate how ill he was. He was spending a fair amount of time in psychotherapy then and I know my mother tried to explain to me why. I observed the countless disputes between them, the shouting matches, and the angry public displays. However, I was young and didn't really understand the full dimensions of what was going on. These hostilities never turned me away from him, as they did to my brother. More than anything, I think I was simply filled with sympathy for him.

In violation of all the canons of psychoanalysis, his therapist befriended my father. That always was a bit of a mystery to me. One night, we were invited to join his family for dinner at their home. My father was deeply depressed then and it was a difficult evening of awkward conversation. I remember we listened to Schubert piano sonatas. Afterwards, the analyst gave me his copy of the record and signed the cover "Music for the soul." I replayed the record countless times and kept it until eventually it began to sound like sandpaper.

My father loved horse racing and each year that he was able, he would take us to the Santa Anita and Hollywood Park race tracks near Los Angeles. Once, he invited his analyst to join us. That was a much happier time. The therapist, in good Freudian fashion, carefully observed the horses as they were parading in front of the grandstand on their way to the starting gate. Those who pooped well were judged to be in excellent condition, whereupon he left to place his bets. I recall he made a good deal of money that day.

I liked bantering with my father's analyst. For some reason, we seemed to hit it off. It was my first experience of "clicking" with someone. This has been a rare experience in my life. I think I would have clicked with my father. Most everyone else did, including his analyst. But, I never really had a chance to find out. This is true for most everything about his life. I was never able to talk with him about his childhood, his first marriage, which I only learned about by chance, as I was thumbing through an old dictionary of his one day. I asked my mother about the bookplate with the name of Edith upon it. She told me it was his first wife and that their marriage had lasted less than a year. I didn't then or ever again pursue the matter further, although now it occurs to me I would have liked to.

My father drank heavily at various times in his life. It was difficult to be with him then, especially for my mother who had to bear the brunt of his emotional outbursts, although they were never violent or physically harmful. It was only much later that I began to study what was known about alcoholism and manic-depressive psychosis, as it was known then. Most of what I read never helped me to better understand his torments or do anything to help him. Neither psychoanalytic therapy, the drugs available at that time, electroshock treatment, or the best private "rest homes," gave him any lasting relief.

Would the newer drugs and treatments available today have made a difference? Perhaps they might have made it easier for him to manage his demons more effectively or put them at a greater distance. However, I am not at all sure about this. I saw the world in which he grew up, the way his mother and father treated him and how he had to spend his working days in the family business. It was never a placid situation. There was no escaping the world he brought with him or the one he had to live through during his all-too-brief life.

In my naive way, I wanted to try to understand what could be done to help him. To some extent, and maybe more than I realized, a fair amount of my time in psychology was devoted to that task. Every now and then, I thought I had come across a useful concept. But by then there was nothing I or anyone else could do with the information.

The most illuminating insight I ever had about what he must have been going through came from an experience when I was recovering from sodium penathol, the anesthetic given to me when I had my wisdom teeth removed. Even though he was quite depressed then, my father was with me in the recovery room. In coming out of the drug, I went through a prolonged period of uncontrollable crying—apparently a not-uncommon aftereffect of that drug. Yet all the while I was fully conscious of my state, and fully aware that no matter how hard I tried, there was nothing I could do to stop. I recall saying to him in my stupor that I knew exactly what he was going through.

My father never knew what ever became of me. Perhaps he would have been a little bit pleased. Nor did he ever come to know my wife. He did meet her once before our marriage, just briefly, during a time when he was very ill and, along with my mother, had come to visit me at college to celebrate my 21st birthday. Afterwards I recall him saying, "She has heart." It was what he always said about the people he really cared for.

How much I envy the young men and women whose father has a continuing presence in their adult life. It has been said that a son's relationship with his father shapes in subtle ways his adult personality and the relationships he forms in adulthood. I have often wondered if I would have done anything different in my life or been a different person had my father not been so ill and had he been alive during my adulthood.

What happens to men who lose their father? I am not thinking of the fatherless young children about which there is so much concern and speculation today. Rather, I mean the young adult men, say between 20-30 years of age who, like myself, were raised by their father but then spend the rest of their life confronted by the gaping emptiness of his death.

The question has been puzzling me for many years now. How is it possible to find out about the effects of something that never happened? At times, I have been ambivalent about my work and social relations. These feelings are sometimes said to occur in men who have not been close to their father. However, I always felt very close to my father and so this idea does not help me much. In addition, I know of men who are far more resolute than I am who often fought bitterly with their father.

My father was never there to pass judgment on what I did. Nor did my mother, for that matter. I used to go about my days rarely thinking of what they or anyone else might think about the choices I made. Occasionally it got me into trouble. But never enough to bother me. Yet many times in my life I have taken the easy route, aborted a chosen path.

After he died, I left graduate school for a while before eventually returning for my doctorate. After receiving it, I resigned from the first job offer I had, only weeks before the academic year began. And I also left the position I devoted most of my life to well before most academics do. Above all, I was never entirely satisfied with my work in psychology or the discipline in general.

Would I have been more decisive, less ambivalent if my father had been a presence in my life? We hear much doubt expressed today about the direct impact of parents on their children's personality and adult behavior, indeed, whether or not they matter at all or matter as much as their peers. It is said, for example, that parental influence on their children has been overestimated. Studies of identical twins (reared apart or together) are cited to show that genetic factors control about half of a person's intellect and personality. Other studies of fatherless children are said to be consistent with this evidence. Rearing a child without an adult male in the household appears to have very little *particular* impact on children. Instead, factors associated with income, frequency of moving, and peer relationships are said to matter more.

My own feeling is that these claims say less about the influence of parents on their children and far more about the methods used to obtain the evidence, especially the methods used to assess adult behavior and personality. Frankly, I do not believe these methods tap the important dimensions of human personality and intellectual ability. Nor do I think the findings have a very high degree of generality. Do they apply to me? The question is unanswerable. There is simply no procedure for determining for whom the findings hold and for whom they don't.

I also believe whatever influence parents have on their children is not likely to be very specific. Instead, we learn from them *very general aspects of character and motivation*. We learn to value learning, not any particular discipline. We see what it means to be generous and helpful, not any particular instance of these acts. In short, our parents provide exemplars for those deeper aspects of human character and feeling that we find are expressed in the sort of persons we become.

By way of example, my father used a great many expressions that you rarely hear today. Like "ribbing" and "honky dory," "okey-dokey," "lollapalooza" and "Let's put the show on the road." Every family has their own private vocabulary and those were some of his favorite expressions, expressions that have remained a part of my ordinary vocabulary to this day. I have come to believe that the indirect and quite unintentional way this occurred to me illustrates the more general process by which parents shape the behavior of their children.

Strangely, I find that the memories that I have of my father grow in clarity with each passing year, no doubt because they are often rehearsed. I recall the mornings we were together when he drove me to school on his way to work. I remember the many long afternoons my mother, brother, and I sat with him in the afternoon sun, watching the Hollywood Stars play baseball at Gilmore Field. I can see him, bald and heavyset, smoking his cigar, my mother keeping score, and my brother and I munching peanuts, mitts in hand, hoping to catch a fly ball that might be hit our way.

My father was a great joker, yet the jokes he told never ended with a punch line. Rather they were short quips, quips that were unexpected and altogether original. They simply emerged while he was bantering or jesting with another person, not the sort that could ever be retold.

I recall how much he enjoyed the radio comedians of the day: Jack Benny, Fred Allen, and Edgar Bergen. We would sit by the radio every Sunday night listening to their shows. And then when television came, doing the same with Milton Berle, Sid Ceasar and above all, Jackie Gleason, who he was much like in appearance and big-heartedness. Each Saturday night, we would sit side by side in our living room armchairs, rolling with laughter at those remarkable Gleason skits.

I visualize him sitting at the head of our dining room table during yet another family gathering, joined by grandparents, numerous aunts and uncles and cousins. And I recall the times he and my grandfather went for a walk after dinner, both smoking their cigars, strolling along the streets of our neighborhood, chatting away the evening. I am grateful they asked me to come along, even though I'm sure I rarely said a word the entire time we were together.

I am often reminded of those times and know that, while they took place many years ago, they continue to play a role in my life. In recalling them, I am reminded of other experiences and times that we were together. They are mostly cheerful times, not the turbulent ones that I have dwelled on here. I did know him for a while. He would have been over ninety now. That is impossible for me to imagine. I only know the robust, yet melancholy person in the memories that come my way each day.

A JOURNEY IN
PSYCHOLOGY

. . . Schopenhauer said that he learned more psychology from Dostoyevsky than from all the books he had read on the subject.[53]

Not long after I embarked on the study of psychology, a vague feeling of dissatisfaction with the field began to take hold of me. It took me a while before I realized why I felt this way, but eventually I came to understand that it was due to the limited ability of the discipline to capture the emotional truths of ordinary experience. While I have great respect for its application of the experimental method and have observed its successes in some areas, I have to confess that much of what passes for psychological research today seems trivial and of little consequence to me.

I have come to this view after a lifetime of schooling that has continued almost without a break since I was 5 years old and, during the last forty years of my life, has been largely devoted to the study of psychology. In the beginning I was student, then a researcher and after that a teacher, and then sometimes all three. These days I also do a little of each with unpredictable frequency.

However, at this point in my life, I have more or less given up on psychology, at least its current versions and preoccupations. I try to keep up with the literature and maintain subscriptions to the leading journals. But I rarely find much of anything that I care to read, as each new issue brings yet another batch of quantitative analyses of esoteric processes that, in most instances, seem remote from human experience. Instead, my interests have turned to literature now, for that is where I find the truths that I do not find in psychology or anywhere else for that matter.

Before I went to college, I had not given much thought to my future. But after my first year at Stanford, I was certain that I didn't want to stray far from the academy. In those days, Stanford freshmen took a full-year course in the history of Western Civilization and then often followed it with another in the Humanities that was devoted to literature and the arts. Those courses introduced me to the world of culture and I've never recovered from the experience or found an alternative that even comes close. Critics who decry the "narrow" Western focus of courses like this would deny undergraduates an incomparable educational experience, one that has little to do with their content and much more with a way of thinking. At least it was a way of thinking that was completely foreign to me at that time, as I suspect it still is for most students today.

Those courses led me to the study of philosophy, which soon became my major, although I was far from well prepared for its rigors. However, I did understand the questions and was much taken by its quest for clarity, which was the dominant concern of the analytic philosophers of the day. The students also impressed me. They were bright, intense, so unlike those I had known before and I hoped that by associating with them, some of their intelligence would rub off on me.

However, when it was time to enter graduate school, I began to have my doubts about philosophy. It was plainly not making much headway in answering questions that it had been considering for ages. Frankly, I was not entirely convinced it was even a goal. It was enough to simply clarify their meaning. Psychology seemed more promising. It had a method for investigating the questions and procedures for deciding between competing answers. I was also attracted by its experimental method that seemed to me to hold out the hope that, at long last, some progress could be made in resolving those perennial philosophical issues.

I did most of my graduate work in the experimental psychology of learning and motivation, where I sought to test Freudian hypotheses in the laboratory. Like many beginning psychology students, Freud's analysis of mental processes appealed to me, as did the importance of early experience in his accounts of adult behavior. Anxiety also played a central role in his theory of the neuroses and because I was young and beset with all the anxieties of youth, I was often preoccupied with the strenuous and usually unsuccessful effort to deal with it. What an excellent topic to study, I thought.

So, in the manner of a clinician, I set about to try to find a way to conquer anxiety. However, my studies were carried out in the laboratory, rather than the clinic. The research employed an animal model of human anxiety, an approach that was highly regarded at the time. Through a series of experiments, I eventually developed a technique that successfully reduced anxiety responses in animals, one that was not unlike a closely related clinical procedure later adopted by behavior therapists. In those days, there was a good deal of interest on the part of clinicians in applying findings derived from animal models in therapeutic settings, a practice that has all but disappeared today.

I continued to pursue learning theory once I began teaching, primarily within the conditioning framework developed by B. F. Skinner. I was always attracted to Skinner's views and research methods, which stressed the study of single organisms in tightly controlled experimental conditions. Using this technique, Skinner sought to develop a set of laws that could predict and control human and animal behavior. While his *deterministic behavioral* model received considerable support at the time, most psychologists eventually came to believe that it could not adequately deal with mental processes and, in due course, it was supplanted by the so-called cognitive revolution, which continues to dominate the field to this day.

However, I was content working within the Skinnerian framework. I welcomed its emphasis on the environmental control of behavior, which I felt was consistent with the weight Freud gave to early experience. I had no trouble employing rigorous laboratory methods or focusing on the behavior of single subjects. Moreover, in the beginning it was exciting to be teaching and doing research with the undergraduate students who came to Reed College, a small liberal arts college in Oregon. I was young, the youngest member of the department, and they were only slightly younger, intelligent, energetic, and a bit nutty, as is often the case at Reed.

They were also attracted by the research I was doing. If I was interested in it, so were they. My lab was crowded, as were my classes. Every once in a while, I would return to my office in the evening, only to be sidetracked by a group of students still working in the lab. It was pretty heady stuff. Looking back on it now, it seems inconceivable—I was studying problems in animal conditioning and the students wanted to work with me.

During the energy crises of the seventies, I began to appreciate the shortcomings of the behavioral approach. I thought profligate energy consumption on the part of individual consumers played a large role in bringing on this crisis and that, while the behavioral approach worked well in producing short-term reductions in energy consumption, the research demonstrated over and over again that these changes never lasted very long. The behavioral account was severely limited in this respect.

About this time, I read some remarkable experiments conducted by Stanley Milgram that set me on the path of understanding this shortcoming. Milgram's classic experiments on obedience and disobedience to authority stunned me. They revealed, in a way, that the behavioral approach never did have the enormous power of the social situation in controlling behavior. They also did this in a compelling laboratory situation of deep personal consequence to the participants. Finally, their relevance to the Holocaust moved me deeply. Countless other students and scholars to this day have been similarly affected by the force of these experiments.

Milgram's program of research turned my interests sharply in the direction of social psychology, a subject that I had never studied before. There I found a provocative body of knowledge on techniques for changing behavior, techniques that relied more on internal rather than external control (rewards and punishments) that was advocated by behavioral analysts. In turn, this suggested a number of applications for promoting energy conservation, as well as other resource-conserving behaviors. As a result, my students and I carried out a program of research within this framework during the next several years.

Naturally, all this eventually came to an end. Younger people came into the department. Their views were new and more in line with the current direction that psychology was taking. Animal conditioning became a thing of the past, indeed, subject to considerable objection on the part of critics. The energy crisis faded away. My lectures became stale. I wasn't learning anything new so my interest in the subject matter flagged and the students no longer seemed interested in my methodical analysis of psychological problems. And so, gradually, I withdrew from the academic fray.

As the years went by, I also lost confidence that psychology could ever become a science of human behavior, at least a science that could speak with any degree of precision about the richness of human experience. Perhaps that was too much to ask of the discipline, too much to ask at this time in its evolution. Yet, I never accepted the claim that psychology was still a young science and that as it matured, some of these limitations would be overcome. In my lifetime, I really didn't see anything to indicate that this was happening. Quite to the contrary, all I could see was growing conflict between theoretical accounts, increasing physiologizing of the field, and continuing contradictions between empirical investigations.

Others have expressed similar views. For example, Rom Harre, researcher, teacher, and writer in the philosophy of science, and later in social psychology has written:

> It has been about 30 years since the first rumblings of discontent with the state of academic psychology began to be heard.... It is a remarkable feature of mainstream academic psychology that, alone among the sciences, it should be almost wholly immune to critical appraisal as an enterprise. Methods that have long been shown to be ineffective or worse are still used on a routine basis by hundreds, perhaps thousands of people. Conceptual muddles long exposed to view are evidence in almost every issue of standard psychology journals.[54]

Geoffrey Loftus, a leading cognitive psychologist, has also spoken of his concerns about the field.

> But I have developed a certain angst over the intervening 30-something years, a constant nagging sensation that our field spends a lot of time spinning its wheels without really making much progress.[55]

Most recently, in a call for greater unity within the field, the current President of the American Psychological Association, Phillip Zimbardo, expressed his concern by writing:

> Psychology continues to be a sea of professional disciplines, rarely connected with each other, loose from any common theoretical moorings, and rarely within sight of the shores of the "real world."[56]

Psychologists seek to establish very general laws of human thought and action. Yet I never understood how evidence derived by averaging the scores of a group of individuals could serve as the foundation for a science of *individual* behavior. Laws based on such aggregate data tell us very little about specific individuals and serve only to obscure crucial features of human variability and uniqueness.

Further, the many exceptions to these laws severely limit their generality. Thus, it is impossible to say with much confidence that they hold for a particular individual at a particular time and place. I have come to believe that psychology will always have to be content with this sort of limitation. Laws based on group means hold for some people, some of the time, but one never can be sure on any given occasion if they apply to a particular individual in the situation at hand.

As a case in point, consider the nature of psychological research on the impact of media violence. This is an important social and personal issue, one in which psychologists have been called upon to provide the kind of evidence that will count in public policy discussions of the matter. After years of research in both laboratory and field situations, it is almost universally accepted that exposure to media violence increases aggressive behavior.

At the same time, it is essential to recognize that there are many important studies in both settings that do not support this claim. It would be more accurate to say that exposure to media violence is not sufficient to produce aggressive behavior. It may teach some persons how to behave aggressively. But individuals simply do not perform everything they learn. Whether or not a person will perform what he or she has learned depends on many factors, most of which have little to do with what they have observed and far more with conditions in their immediate environment—they have had a bad day at the office, been insulted by a close friend, been involved in an automobile accident, etc.

Above all, there are important individual differences in responsiveness to media violence. Obviously, such exposure does not affect everyone in the same way. The observation of media violence may have an immediate, short-term effect on some individuals. But almost all the studies agree that these effects do not last very long.

In short, exposure to media violence *may* affect only a very few individuals for a very short time under very limited conditions. The question then becomes who and under what circumstances? And if media violence does only influence a few on those occasions, what are the social policy implications of this conclusion, especially when it is impossible to predict who will be influenced in this way?

This conclusion is not unlike one often voiced in judicial proceedings, where the legal standing of psychological research is also called into question. It took me a while to understand why courts were so hesitant to admit social science evidence, let alone take it seriously in adjudicating cases. Yet legal cases are decided on an *individual* basis and so, even when the weight of evidence clearly supports the relevant social science generalization, the courts still require "proof" that it applies in the case being decided. When judges ask psychologists to link the general principle to the specific case, it is difficult, if not impossible for them to do so with certainty. But that is what the law requires. Psychologists can provide relevant case knowledge and guidance, but the information they present is rarely, if ever, decisive in judicial decision-making.

In his essay Medicine and Literature, Robert Coles puts the matter eloquently.

> I am constantly impressed with mystery, and maybe even feel that there are certain things than cannot be understood or clarified through generalizations, that resolve themselves into matters of individuality, and again, are part of the mystery of the world that one celebrates as a writer, rather than tries to solve and undo as a social scientist .... As physicians we also know, or ought to know, that each person is different, each patient reacts in his or her special way to any illness, and indeed to life itself. A sense of complexity of human affairs, a respect for human particularity, ... these are the stuff of the humanities at their best ... [57]

During all the time I was primarily engaged in psychology, I never stopped reading literature, mostly contemporary fiction. I did not have the time to read widely, but the literature I did read always seemed to be telling me things about myself and others that I never heard expressed in psychology. With rare exceptions, I rarely saw individuals in psychology as clearly or as deeply as I did in the novels and short stories that I read.

Several years ago, I started to record the passages that conveyed these literary truths in the books and stories that I read. Some had a great many, while others had none. I tend to judge the quality of a literary work by the number of passages that I have taken the trouble to record. At the end of each year, I make a copy of the collection and place it in my journal. The computer has made all this possible. In the days before I had one, I don't remember doing anything like this. Perhaps I wrote a phrase or a sentence in long hand, but never very many and never as extensively as I do now.

While some are simply amusing or witty expressions, the majority convey a truth that I've not been aware of or seen so clearly expressed before. Sometimes the passages reinforce a belief I already hold and then at other times, it is a truth that I've always wanted to hear or hoped I would, even though I may not have been able to articulate it myself.

In his book, *Existential Psychology*, Irving Yalom wrote perceptively about these special truths of literature:

> Great literature survives, as Freud pointed
> out in his discussion of *Oedipus Rex* because
> something in the reader leaps out to embrace

its truth. The truth of fictional characters moves us because it is our own truth. Furthermore, great works of literature teach us about ourselves because they are scorchingly honest, as honest as any clinical data: the great novelist . . . is ultimately highly self-revelatory. Thornton Wilder once wrote: If Queen Elizabeth or Frederick the Great or Ernest Hemingway were to read their biographies, they would exclaim, "Ah— my secret is still safe." But if Natasha Rostov were to read *War and Peace* she would cry out, as she covered her face with her hands, "How did he know? How did he know?"

Phyllis Rose expresses a similar view in her recent book on Marcel Proust.[58]

. . . but what I looked forward to most in reading Proust were revelations about myself. The best moments had been those in which I descended most deeply into myself . . . so I achieved a sudden clarity of vision . . . . Proust understood that every reader, in reading, reads himself. Far from minding this, he saw it as the writer's task to facilitate it. Thus, the writer's word is merely a kind of optical instrument, which he offers to the reader to enable him to discern what, without this book he would perhaps never have perceived in himself. And the recognition by the reader in his own self of what the book says is *proof of its veracity*. [Italics mine]

Here Rose suggests that the power of literature lies in confirming those truths of experience that are unique to each individual. These are truths that are not to be found in the pursuit of generalities, but rather in the conditions of our own lives. I think an idiographic science of the individual is possible, a science that is occasionally revealed in psychological research, but far more often in those unforgettable passages of literature that we are lucky enough to stumble upon.

I respect the effort of psychologists to understand the world and render it in some lawful fashion. I am grateful for the chance that I was given to study the discipline and for those times when it set me to thinking. But this work has taught me to be wary of generalizations about human beings and to value instead the truths of individual experience.

This is why, as I come to the last leg of my life, I have decided to make a turn to literature and to the pleasure of putting words, instead of numbers, on the page. I have no expectations of being able to achieve any distinction as a writer. But there are times when nothing can hold a candle to it; to say nothing of the way it helps get me through the day.

Notes

53 Interviewer's comment during interview with Julian Barnes, *Paris Review* #157, Winter 2OOO-2001.

54 Rom Harre (2000 August 25). Acts of living. *Science*, 289, 1303-1304.

55   Geofrrey Loftus. Psychology will be a much better science when
     we change the way we analyze data. *Current Directions in
     Psychological Science*, 1996, 5, 151-171

56   Phillip Zimbardo. President's Column, *Monitor on Psychology*,
     March, 2002.

57   Robert Coles, *Times of Surrender*. Iowa City: University of Iowa
     Press. 1988.

58   Phyllis Rose, *The Year of Reading Proust*. Washington, D.C.:
     Counterpoint Press. 2000